OUT ON A LIMB

Out on a Limb

A Branch Campus Life

CHARLES P. BIRD, PHD

Encore Dreams, LLC
encoredreams.com
© 2014 by Charles P. Bird
All rights reserved

Charles P. Bird
Encore Dreams, LLC
P.O. Box 5604
Athens, OH 45701

Printed in the United States of America
This book is printed on acid-free paper ∞™

24 23 22 21 20 19 18 17 16 15 14   5 4 3 2 1

Paperback ISBN: 978-0-9914982-0-8

Electronic ISBN: 978-0-9914982-1-5

*To the angels in my life, beginning with my
mother, my father, and my wife and sons, then
reaching out across the years and miles to so
many who encouraged me when I most needed
encouragement, challenged me when I lost
focus, and above all brought a sense of purpose
and joy into a life that has been truly blessed.*

Contents

Preface

Nearly my entire professional career has involved working with university branch campuses. Toward the end of my full-time work, I became involved in the development and marketing of online programs, which broadened my perspective in many ways. Eventually, I came to think of myself as something of a specialist in programs for adult learners, but my deepest commitment has been, and is still, to expanding access and opportunity for people who otherwise might have little hope of attaining their educational dreams.

The areas that have attracted my professional interest and personal commitment also are of particular significance at present. For a variety of financial and strategic reasons, many institutions of higher education have become more concerned about their ability to attract and retain adult learners. In my opinion, most presidents, provosts, and deans, accustomed to thinking in more traditional terms, tend to miss the mark when it comes to recruiting students who are thought of as "nontraditional."

Moreover, the world of higher education has become increasingly competitive and affected by the impact of technology. The times call for innovation and entrepreneurship, especially in the very areas that are served by branch campuses and online programs. Only the most uninformed observer would suggest that traditional institutions are prepared to respond effectively to the current challenges, although I could point to a few examples of presidents around the country who clearly get it.

Despite the fact that much has been written about adult learners and online programs, there has been relatively little attention to the role of branch campuses. The literature is sparse in part because branches have developed idiosyncratically, in response to differing local circumstances. Nevertheless, across more than thirty-five years of work as a faculty member, an administrator, and, more recently, a consultant, as I have visited dozens of branches and met hundreds of people who work on branches, I have found similarities in their concerns and generalizations that can be made about how they grow and thrive.

In that context, I offer this book, hoping that it may tell a reasonably interesting story, at least for those who work on or with branch campuses. More important, I hope it provides a broad perspective on branch campus life. I make no claim of special wisdom here. I've simply been around a long time, paid attention during that time, and had more opportunities than most to learn about various approaches.

Each chapter is more or less independent of the others, although it may be important to read chapter 2 before reading those that come later, and chapter 10 may make more sense after reading most of the rest of the book. To document my bona fides, chapter 1 is directly autobiographical, but throughout the book I draw heavily on my personal experience. Chapters 4 to 9 relate more or less closely to what was on my mind at various stages of my career, from faculty member, to associate dean, to dean, to vice president.

You will not find a lot of references in this book. That is partly because there isn't a great deal of research that I felt would be helpful, but it also ties to the fact that I wanted to tell a story, not write a scholarly treatise. I'd like to think that what I have to say is well informed, but that is for the reader to judge. I'd be very pleased to learn that some of what I have to say encourages others to do some serious research, whether it confirms what I have to say, or not.

I also want to be clear that I make no claims of originality with regard to anything I write. I have learned from so many people, not to mention from constant reading. At this point, I rarely know where I picked up an idea, and I apologize if anyone feels that I've failed to acknowledge his or her thoughts. Somewhere along the line, I just found telling stories to be more interesting, but I hope I generally keep my feet on the ground.

As a final note, I actually have been a bit dismayed to see an increase in reporting by higher education newsletters that purports to address "branch campuses." In most cases, however, the articles have been about elite American universities that are opening branches in foreign countries. Often, the stories use the term "branch campus" as if it *meant* "campus in a foreign location." There also has been a more interesting story (at least to me) about private nonprofit universities locating branches in states that are at a considerable distance from the home institutions. In this book, these topics, while not irrelevant, are not addressed directly.

For all that, I do want to acknowledge some people whose friendship or professional connection has mattered most to me. I was fortunate to work closely with a number of people I think of as mentors, including the two men to whom I reported before becoming a vice president, John Riedl and Jim Bryant; I learned so much from each of them. I was especially fortunate to work closely with two presidents, Robert Glidden and Roderick McDavis, and several provosts, including Kathy Krendl, Sharon Brehm, and Gary Shoemaker.

More broadly, I am grateful for faculty colleagues who enriched my life, stayed friends through ups and downs, and also taught me important lessons. Here, I think of David Scott, Terri Fisher, Raymond Dominick, Ted Dahlstrand, Tim Berra, and many others. At Ohio University, I developed strong friendships with

Leonard Raley, Gary Neiman, and other vice presidents or deans, and I continue to value their perspectives on life and work.

I deeply value my relationship with the people who reported to me on an organizational chart, but whom I think of today as being friends, even more than colleagues. The names are too many to list, but I hope they know how much they continue to mean to me. Special mention goes to Bill Willan, Steve Flaherty, Tom Shostak, Dan Evans, John Furlow, Linda Lockhart, Debbie Catri, and Kim Hayden.

Then, there are people who are friends first, but from whom I also have received professional support: Susan Ringer, Christine Quinn, Ken Shaw, Brenda Harms, Yvonne Ulmer, Jenny Hegland, Randy Leite, and Cindy Wheatley, among others.

Support and encouragement from family may be the most important of all. I can never express the depth of my gratitude, beginning with my parents, but extending to a remarkable group of grandparents, uncles, aunts, and cousins. My sons, daughters-in-law, and grandchildren enrich my life beyond words, bringing a sort of pure joy that leaves me feeling truly blessed. More than anyone, however, my wife, Gail, has been there through good times and bad, given me the space to pursue my adventures, and made my life easier in countless large and small ways.

Finally, I want to acknowledge and express appreciation to several people without whom this book would likely have remained a series of blog posts: my friend and the former director of the Ohio University Press, David Sanders; my editor, Nancy Basmajian, who did much to improve the manuscript; and Beth Pratt, who handled design and production for the final book.

1

A Partial Memoir

I FLEW FROM TALLAHASSEE TO COLUMBUS in April 1976 to interview for a faculty position at Ohio State's Mansfield regional campus. Jobs were scarce, as they often seem to be, but I felt unsure about pursuing a position at a branch of the "real" university.

I may not have been the sharpest new PhD on the market, but you'd be hard pressed to find anyone more mainstream or traditional in his views. Other than being aware of the fact that universities sometimes have branch campuses, I didn't know anything about them. I did know that I needed a job, because my wife was pregnant and I had been looking for over a year, and I wanted an opportunity to continue developing my research and publication record. I enjoyed teaching, and I liked the idea of being a faculty member at a Big Ten university, but I wanted to learn more about the expectations, opportunities, and fit.

The interview went well, in both Columbus and Mansfield; I received a decent offer and quickly accepted the appointment. I was on the tenure track in one of the strongest psychology departments in the country! My first-year salary was just over $13,000.

More than thirty-five years later, I remain involved with branch campuses. I've never met anyone else who has filled the range of roles that I have, from faculty member, to campus associate dean (responsible for academic and student affairs), to campus dean, to vice president of a system with five campuses and two centers. I've visited branch campuses across the country, often in a consulting role, as well as campuses in Canada, Mexico, and Russia.

THE CONTEXT

If I say that there are 7,000 satellite or branch campuses across the United States, including branches of community colleges, public universities, and private nonprofit institutions, and that they enroll more than five million students, no one can prove me wrong. The fact is that there are no relevant comprehensive statistics on branch campuses. In fact, although there are some decent definitions of types of branches and centers, the terms are not consistently employed, and there is no consistency in how institutions recognize campuses or attribute enrollment.

Alternatively, I might say there are at least 2,500 branches, enrolling more than two million students, and that both campuses and enrollment are expanding more rapidly than in any other sector of traditional, campus-based higher education. Again, I can't prove that is true, other than in very narrow ways, but my best guess is that these are conservative numbers.

Regardless, there is no doubt that a surprisingly large number of students attend various satellites of established institutions, whether we call them branches, regional campuses, centers, or sites. Yet there is almost no literature that can guide institutional leaders in thinking about best practices; making decisions on facilities, staffing, oversight, or budgets; or developing a solid business plan to support the launch of a new effort.

In the absence of significant resources, this book is based mostly on my own experiences and observations, as well as what I've learned from others. My academic interests are in social and organizational behavior, and I've tried to think about my experiences in that context.

Still, I need to acknowledge what many branch campus folks know to be true: My positions have been at public research universities, and even though I know people at other types of institutions, and I've thought seriously about the issues that affect branches, this account is based on my personal experience. The range of branch experiences is as varied as the range of any other type of educational institution.

FIRST STEPS

I obtained my bachelor's degree in psychology at Virginia Tech. Beginning in my junior year, I worked as an undergraduate research assistant, and I thoroughly enjoyed the experience. Accordingly, I applied to graduate school and enrolled at Florida State University, in experimental psychology.

My specialty was human learning and memory. Although I had some early success with my research, toward the end of my doctoral program I realized that I needed teaching experience. I decided to participate in a teaching "externship" program that the department offered, and I went off to spend a semester at Valencia Community College, in Orlando.

At Valencia, I taught four sections of general psychology and discovered that I really enjoyed teaching. Now, I felt ready for a career! (The truth is that I tend to enjoy new experiences, so my career has often involved getting into new things and becoming excited about the opportunities.) Most of my friends were landing at small private institutions, with heavy undergraduate teaching loads and only modest research expectations. I assumed the same thing would likely happen to me, and I made my peace with the notion of a career dedicated to that type of mission.

Thus, when the opportunity came to work at Ohio State, even on a branch campus, I was pleased. My salary was slightly higher than what most of my friends were receiving, and the teaching load, although heavy by Columbus standards, was lighter than at most teaching-intensive institutions. Importantly, the institutional culture supported a level of research activity that I wanted.

At Ohio State, unlike at many institutions, my rank and tenure were in the psychology department. That was a major attraction to me, because it provided a natural line of communication with colleagues in the department. My hope and intention was to work in Mansfield for a few years, generate more publications, and move on.

With experience and hindsight, I realize that I was very fortunate, compared to many new faculty members. In addition to my teaching experience at Valencia, I stayed on a year in Tallahassee, post-PhD, teaching at both Florida State and Florida A&M. When I arrived at Ohio State, I had already taught eleven sections of general psychology, and I had experience with other courses that was helpful. I had begun to discover my teaching style, as well as how to pace a course, how to prepare exams, and the like.

I was fortunate not only that my dissertation research was published in one of the top-tier journals for my specialty, but that it led directly to a series of additional studies. Thus, when I arrived in Mansfield, I had two post-dissertation articles in press, and I knew exactly what the next experiments would be. I was ready to move ahead, toward tenure.

I'm sure that most branch campus faculty members arrive less prepared to meet the expectations of a research university. At least at Ohio State and Ohio, although the expectations for research and publication are significantly lower at branch campuses than at the main campus, the teaching loads are higher and, generally, less directly relevant to the faculty member's need to stay current in his or her discipline. Facilities are less conducive to research, graduate assistants are usually unavailable, and service expectations are typically at least modestly higher than the levels many main campus assistant professors face.

I had still another good break when I arrived at Ohio State. My office was located next to that of a senior, highly respected faculty member, who embodied the balance of teaching, research, and service required of an Ohio State branch campus faculty member. This physics professor, David Scott, became something of a mentor and a good friend. In addition, a couple of main campus colleagues included me in meetings and on thesis committees that helped keep me in the loop of scholars in my own specialty.

It is interesting to reflect on the fact that serving on a branch campus almost always implies lower status than serving on the main campus. Yet, if the match between a person's interests and personality and the mission of the institution is on target, then career growth and satisfaction seems more likely. For me, I feel certain that it was a lucky thing that I landed on a branch campus. But it took me a while to figure that out.

Looking back, I can see that I always had broad interests in psychology and related disciplines. At one time or another I taught nearly all of what psychology professors would recognize as the broad survey courses in our field (social, developmental, adjustment, abnormal, industrial/organizational, etc.). I explored the psychology of consciousness and offered a special topics course on that subject, even as I taught behavior modification and theories of learning.

Eventually, working on a branch campus led me to examine and change my area of interest from learning and memory to social and organizational behavior. Would that have occurred to me, if I had been working on the main campus of a research university? Would the expectations for publication, commitments to graduate students and colleagues, or investments in laboratory equipment have limited my perspective or opportunity? I just don't know. However, here is what happened:

I had been teaching social psychology from the time of my arrival in Mansfield, and I became intrigued by the research questions in that area. I was especially drawn to research on attitudes, attribution theory, and interpersonal relationships. In addition, although I was able to attract bright undergraduate students to assist me in data collection for my memory research, that field is so esoteric that I rarely had opportunities to teach at a level that had any connection to my research.

A few years into my faculty career, needing extra money, I responded to calls from community organizations asking me to speak (for a small fee) to their groups. The topics were nearly always applied, and the audiences were engaged and fun. I realized that speaking to groups outside the typical classroom, with no exams or essential principles to cover, was satisfying and a refreshing complement to my usual experience.

At about that time, our continuing education office invited me to teach an American Management Association course on memory improvement. The students in this noncredit class were mostly working, experienced managers. The course proved to be fun and positively challenging. One of my students was personnel manager for a local firm, and he asked me to do a series of presentations on topics in organizational behavior for his management group. I was nervous about all this, because I was uncertain about my knowledge in these areas, but it ended up being another good experience.

As a result, I began to read more systematically in the area of organizational behavior (work motivation, decision making, change and conflict management, leadership, and so on). The topics were reasonably related to social psychology, and sometimes my knowledge of learning theory and human information processing gave me a unique twist on the topics. I also approached two industrial/organizational (I/O) psychology colleagues on the Columbus campus, Milt Hakel and Rich Klimoski, who were helpful in advising me on my self-guided exploration of their field.

So, at this point, my professional life was getting more than a little bizarre. I was conducting laboratory research in human short-term memory, teaching mostly applied psychology courses, and like a double agent with a secret identity, going off to present various programs to area business and professional groups. Keeping up with reading memory research, reading for my classes, and reading to develop my expertise in I/O psychology was too much. Moreover, I was assuming more leadership responsibilities on the faculty, which created still more demands on my time.

I remember going home one afternoon and doing something I've done several times over the years. I sat on my bed, with a pad of paper, and began to list all of my activities and interests. I looked for a way to align my work so that it felt more comfortable and positive. Ultimately, I decided to commit to industrial-organizational psychology. I saw potential synergies across teaching, research, and community service, and I thought that type of work might open new opportunities in the future.

Without a doubt, working on a regional campus made it easier to redirect my career. With support and advice from colleagues, I shifted my teaching to emphasize social psychology and I/O psychology, and I sought and received approval to teach the required organizational behavior course in the business curriculum.

All this created a change of direction that was a little scary in some ways, but it worked out well. I enjoyed the classes, which helped renew my enthusiasm for teaching. I expanded the range of my management workshops and very much enjoyed that form of teaching, which also gave me opportunities to learn about other types of organizations. Although my new research projects lacked the programmatic quality of my memory work, I did manage to continue publishing steadily in good journals.

It was apparent to me by this point that I would not likely find a faculty position at another university. Although I was admitted to the graduate faculty and served on some master's thesis committees, I simply did not have the kinds of achievements that major research departments would want; but as a tenured faculty member at Ohio State, smaller schools couldn't offer the salary and benefits that I enjoyed. I expected that I would continue to reinvent myself from time to time, seeking new things to do, but that my future would be in Mansfield.

MOVING INTO ADMINISTRATION

In late 1986, the Mansfield dean and director (chief administrator) resigned suddenly. This dean had served for only ten months, but during that time the campus had experienced considerable turmoil, and the associate dean left for another institution. John Riedl, who was sent by Provost Myles Brand to lead the campus after the dean's resignation, asked me to serve as acting associate dean.

Although I had considered administration as a career option, I had also decided I did not want to give up being a professor. (I always appreciated the flexibility and control of my time that being a faculty member allowed.) On the other hand, I was uncomfortable with the fact that, although participants in my credit and noncredit classes felt I had good insight into management issues, I had no firsthand management experience. Therefore, believing the experience would be good, and hoping that I could make a helpful contribution to moving the campus forward, I decided to accept the opportunity.

Because of the circumstances, my expectation was that my role as associate dean might last about two years. I figured I could do the job that long, get my firsthand management experience, help the campus through a difficult time, and then get back to my teaching and research. That isn't quite the way things worked out.

In the spring of 1987, Provost Brand appointed our "interim dean" as permanent dean and director. Dean Riedl asked me to continue as permanent associate dean, and I agreed, although I still expected to return to the faculty within a few years.

Several things happened to encourage me to stay in administration longer than I had expected. First, because of the circumstances at the campus when I started, my initial experiences were both stimulating and satisfying. I could see that we were making an important difference to the campus. Dean Riedl had been at the university for a long time, and his knowledge allowed him to maneuver better than most through the institutional bureaucracy. He was a strong leader, willing to step up on important issues and to act on strongly held values. He was a remarkably skilled budget person, and I learned a lot from him in that area. For my part, I knew the faculty and the local community. I was able to bring some things to the table that the dean valued, and I could see how my own contributions mattered.

In addition to the stimulation and sense of importance in what we were doing, I discovered that my problem-solving skills were helpful in the role of associate dean. For the first few years, I enjoyed working on our class schedule, and I was able to bring improvements to it that both faculty members and students appreciated. In addition, in his early years, the new dean leaned on me to represent the campus to the business community. (Although I did work with area school systems, the dean was relatively more comfortable in that area, so we essentially divided the community work between the business community and the schools.) Over the years, I had wonderful and challenging opportunities to provide leadership in the Mansfield community, especially with the local mental health board and with the local United Way.

Still another attraction of administrative work was that I discovered real interest and satisfaction in working with classified (hourly) and administrative staff. Within the first two years, I had an opportunity to hire most of the staff that reported to me, and I enjoyed both the management and the coaching/mentoring role. I learned a lot about managing change during this time, as well. I assumed responsibility for student services, student activities, and the library, in addition to handling academic affairs. All of this gave me enough variety and opportunity so that my relatively short attention span didn't become a problem.

Throughout my years in administration, I continued to teach. In Mansfield, I taught organizational behavior every year. Later, when I moved to Ohio University, my teaching shifted back to psychology. Although I did not continue my research, I pursued opportunities to write for newspapers and magazines, as an extension of my management development programs. I continued and expanded the range of those programs, so that I felt, through my credit and noncredit teaching, as well as through my writing and management seminars, that I was engaged in my discipline. I also presented papers at administrative conferences from time to time, often on topics related to organizational behavior.

For the first five years as associate dean, I continued to learn and grow. At that point, I decided I would like to have a chance to be a campus dean, to see what I could do in that job. In addition, I honestly didn't want to go back to full-time teaching. Although I enjoy teaching, I felt that I would miss the variety and challenge of administration, and I didn't want to teach the number of introductory sections I knew I would be assigned.

So, I began a job search. I learned quickly that I could make almost any short list for a branch campus deanship, but I couldn't get even a serious nibble for any other administrative role. I had several interviews, which I enjoyed for the insight they provided into other regional/branch campuses, but it wasn't until the deanship at Ohio University's Lancaster campus came open that I received an offer.

CHANGING INSTITUTIONS

I almost didn't apply for the Lancaster position. Ray Wilkes was dean in Lancaster for seventeen years before his unexpected death. Ray was extremely well respected by branch campus people outside of Ohio University, so I assumed that he would be an impossible act to follow. After a few phone calls, however, I learned that there were some interesting challenges at Lancaster—just the sort of opportunity I wanted. The position also was attractive because I was already in my eighteenth year in the Ohio state retirement system.

Working in Lancaster definitely was a challenge. It is hard to believe that regional campuses at two public universities in the same state can be as different as Mansfield and Lancaster. Two structural differences were especially important. First, faculty members at Ohio State hold their rank and tenure in the main campus department. Letters of offer are signed by both the department chair and the regional campus dean, and the primary vote on tenure and promotion takes place in the department, proceeding to the college dean. At Ohio University, faculty members are tenured on the regional campus, and, especially historically, the departments had relatively little involvement in hiring and promotion/tenure decisions.

In addition, each Ohio State campus is a separate entity. There is no central office, and each dean reports directly to the provost. (Practically, the lines of communication aren't quite that simple, but that's the way things show up on the organizational chart.) At Ohio University, there was a vice president (formerly vice provost) responsible for the campuses. (As I write, the most comparable position carries the title of executive dean, reporting to the provost, instead of the president. More about that later.) Perhaps the biggest implications of this difference between institutions related to budget control and how the regional campuses were represented to the main campus. The overall effect was that campus deans had less autonomy at Ohio University. My responsibility as Lancaster dean felt to me more like a half step than a full step up the ladder from being the Mansfield associate dean, especially considering the degree of independence Dean Riedl had given me to pursue various interests.

I started as dean in Lancaster on February 1, 1995. The very first day on the job we had a search for a philosophy professor go sour, and I found myself caught between the Philosophy Department and my own search committee. I must have had the shortest honeymoon on record.

I won't try to describe the issues in Lancaster in any detail. Enrollment had declined on campus for years, but a relatively large prison program that was ending as I arrived obscured the decline to most people on campus. The budget had been in deficit for at least three years. I felt that the staff, although quite competent, was stale. In addition, the class schedule was driven by priorities that I found strange, and there was a serious lack of trust among faculty members, not to mention between faculty and administration.

When I met with individual faculty members, they spoke with enthusiasm about how much they enjoyed teaching in Lancaster, but then nearly every individual would say something like, "Now, let me tell you my war stories." In sum, I concluded that Lancaster was not a happy place, and its declining enrollment at a time when many branch campuses around Ohio were growing rapidly didn't help. Rightly or wrongly, I decided to challenge both faculty and administration.

Regardless of what individuals may feel about my leadership in Lancaster, the budget was balanced every year I was there. Enrollment increased, we worked hard to empower positive faculty members, and we hired some very good faculty and staff members, I believe. About the time I was leaving, only four years later, a new group of faculty members began to step up as leaders, and the campus continued to do well in critical areas.

One of the projects we initiated while I was in Lancaster was the development of an outreach program in Pickerington, Ohio. Pickerington is essentially a bedroom community for Columbus, and our center there gave us better access to a large metropolitan area. The center grew rapidly, and eventually we opened our own buildings, creating what some people call a twig (a branch of a branch). The Pickerington Center is a nice example of a limited service type of branch, which I will say more about in a later chapter. It also became increasingly successful as a graduate center, offering part-time programs that are easily accessible from across the region.

As I entered my fourth year in Lancaster, I felt that we had begun to turn the corner. However, I also felt that the effort had taken too much emotional energy on my part. I decided that I needed at least to consider moving on. Somewhat to my surprise, I wound up receiving an opportunity to become vice president for Regional Higher Education (RHE) at Ohio University.

SYSTEM LEADERSHIP

Contrary to what I know some people in Lancaster believed, I never expected to be considered for the vice presidency. My attitude in all of my administrative positions was that I would do the things I felt I needed to do, recognizing that by challenging people I might actually close the door to future advancement. I also took care to maintain a lifestyle that could be supported by a nine-month salary, if I ever decided or was asked to return to the faculty. In Mansfield, I had so many supportive colleagues, and the campus was so successful, that I had very few public critics, and none with any real influence. In Lancaster, however, I had much more vocal critics, who tended to personalize their criticism in ways that I thought might be more hurtful to me.

I remember talking with Dean Riedl in Mansfield about what I perceived to be unfair criticism or personal attacks, but I experienced much more of that sort of thing in Lancaster. The only advice I can give other administrators, other than to have a thick skin, is to stay on what I call the "academic high road." Know yourself and your values, be consistent in your message, and your critics may voice their objections but aren't likely to win any long-term gains. On the contrary, most people are willing to listen to you and give you a chance for success.

I did eventually apply for the position of vice president, with encouragement from certain individuals in Athens—and because I couldn't quite figure out where else a vice president for regional higher education would come from. Whoever got the job, if not I, would be my immediate supervisor. I wanted the successful candidate to bring skills or qualities that would make him or her a supervisor I could value and respect.

And so it goes. It was a long process, but on March 29, 1999, I began my duties as vice president for regional higher education. In that position, I was responsible for five regional campuses and the Division of Lifelong Learning. Collectively, the campuses enrolled approximately nine thousand students per quarter, and Lifelong Learning, based on the Athens campus, served many additional students through a variety of credit and noncredit programs, including a long-standing, paper-based array of correspondence courses, still attractive to certain audiences.

I continued to find Ohio University a challenging, sometimes difficult, place to work. I do not feel comfortable going into too many details about the "difficult" part. In his book *The Tipping Point*, Malcolm Gladwell (2000) talks about The Rule of 150. The idea is that a leader can maintain a more or less personal relationship with a maximum of about 150 individuals. The branch campuses where I worked had about 100 employees, including faculty, staff, and adjuncts. It is an ideal size for knowing people, suggesting that a person who is acting with integrity will be less vulnerable to *ad hominem* attacks and can actively participate in the campus dialog.

Moreover, in this era of continuous change and increased competition, a branch campus is sized well for a leader interested in change management. I've said that a campus executive can move the campus forward through the sheer force of his or her vision and energy, assuming support from key institutional leaders. That is not true for a system leader. Having moved to an executive role, I found delegation to be essential, and my removal from so many day-to-day activities meant that I was dependent upon the campus leaders to accomplish our agenda.

As vice president, I was responsible for about 450 employees, in all categories, and nearly all of them were working at least fifty miles away from my office. I got to know many of them, but I found it a constant surprise to discover not only that my views had on occasion been misrepresented, but that people sometimes characterized my motives in ways that I had no effective means to combat. (To keep this in perspective, most academic administrators who work at an executive level have these sorts of experiences, so I don't know that my experience was especially unusual.)

In other ways, however, I had a great experience as vice president. My work with Lifelong Learning opened up some outstanding international opportunities. (Among other things, we had a center in Hong Kong that reported up to me!) I enjoyed being at the table with other executive officers, and the experience made me smarter. I developed a stronger institutional perspective and discovered the strategic pleasures of leading such a large organization.

One of the unexpected benefits of my position derived from the fact that there are not very many institutions where the senior person leading branch campuses holds the title of vice president. It is much more common to be a vice provost, assistant vice president, or the like. The reporting line seems most often to be to the provost, but sometimes it is to an administrative vice president or even a vice president for student affairs. I think the title sometimes opened doors for me, both inside and outside Ohio University.

FINDING A THEME

Sharon Brehm was the provost at Ohio University when I first came to the main campus. Like me, she is a psychologist, and I found our shared language and worldview to be helpful. One of the best pieces of advice she gave me was that I should define and share a "theme" for my time as chief administrator for the campuses.

At an early retreat with the campus deans, the Lifelong Learning dean, and my office staff, I asked the question: "What is it that provides the common link for all of our units?" The emerging answer was a shared mission of outreach and access. (Today, I might prefer access and opportunity.)

From my point of view, mission should always be the driver that helps us set goals and track our progress. Outreach and Access became the RHE theme, and I found that tag line very useful over the years.

The next step was to translate the theme/mission into goals. For a vice president, the goals needed to be relatively broad in scope, to move us ahead in our mission, to assure financial success, and to meet the charge I received from the president when I was hired to strengthen the academic reputation of the campuses.

To be sure, it took more time than in previous positions to get my head around the issues, not to mention the strengths and weaknesses of RHE. The relationships were much more complicated, the budget was much larger, and the politics were more complex. There were enormous differences across the six units for which I was responsible, and the need to build credibility in Athens was important. Nevertheless, eventually I settled on four areas of focus that I wanted to represent the general goals for my time as vice president.

First, we concentrated on strengthening our faculty. The deans and I believed that we needed to offer more opportunities for students to complete baccalaureate degrees on our regional campuses, both to serve our communities and to assure our continued success. Those programs, however, were housed in main campus departments, and because regional faculty members were hired and tenured on the regional campuses, Athens faculty often did not know their regional colleagues. In addition, over the years, there had been too many times that faculty members on regional campuses were "caught" teaching courses for which they lacked approval, or were perceived as not maintaining the standards of the department that "owned" the course. We needed to provide support for faculty development, stronger oversight of the teaching approval process, and clear indications in Athens that RHE was as committed to high academic standards as the main campus was.

Accordingly, we did a number of things to improve our practices, including preparing hiring guidelines, developing more specific promotion and tenure guidelines, and developing a standard dossier format for promotion and tenure cases. Because one of our goals was to raise the standards for professional or scholarly achievements by faculty, we also developed a number of support programs, including load reduction policies, an international travel fund, an undergraduate research support fund, and a research development program that was intended to make participants more competitive for internal and external grants.

Second, we worked hard to strengthen our reputation, both inside and outside the university. I think it is fair to say that some people around the country became aware that we are doing some interesting things at Ohio University, if only judging by the number of phone calls and visits we received. Internally, we tried to be much more visible and to do a better job of telling our story. An "annual report" we created to feature the work of our faculty was well received, and I got a lot of positive feedback on the progress we made.

Third, we tried to encourage more collaboration across the units in RHE and partnerships with units in Athens. The collaboration within RHE occurred only at relatively modest levels, and it remains a disappointment to me. For whatever reasons, I was unable to articulate the importance of collaboration, both to improve the quality of life for faculty and staff members and to maintain important efficiencies, given our size and resources.

Alternatively, perhaps I successfully articulated the value of collaboration but was unable to effectively motivate activity at the level I am convinced was possible.

Partnerships went much better. We built much stronger ties with various academic units across the university; we tried to be good team players with various administrative units. Importantly, the fact that we had an independent budget meant that partnering with RHE could generate much-needed revenue for the academic unit—revenue originating outside the Athens budget process. We were aggressive in using that tool!

Fourth, we strengthened our budget management practices. On the one hand, I gave deans more flexibility in managing their budgets, while also creating more accountability and incentives for good performance. The details of how we approached the budget went through several iterations, but I think we reached a reasonable approach that supported our growth. Most important, enrollment grew, we kept expenses under control, and we built a solid fund balance at a time when Ohio institutions, like so many others across the nation, were experiencing budget cuts from the state. I learned a lot about how to manage budgets, in line with our vision and goals.

One of the most interesting parts of my job was working with the Division of Lifelong Learning (LLL). Through LLL we were responsible for conferences and workshops, independent study (correspondence), summer programs, some international programs, and distance programs. (Our approach to distance programs, at the time, employed a mix of online work and "intensive residencies.")

Although I had been involved in regional campus continuing education programs for a long time, working with LLL gave me responsibility for activities that were quite different from my previous experience. Moreover, LLL inherently relied on partnerships and was engaged in potentially interesting work with Athens academic units. I tried to encourage collaboration between LLL and the regional campuses, but the campuses were not particularly interested and nothing came of it. Some of the initiatives we developed through LLL had potential to take enrollment away from the campuses, so it would have been in their best interest to work together.

FINAL THOUGHTS

Working at Ohio University brought me wonderful opportunities for international experiences. In Lancaster, I had an opportunity to travel to Russia; and my responsibilities in Athens took me to Europe, Mexico, and Asia. During annual visits to our Hong Kong center, I also made side trips to Thailand and to Japan. In addition, I frequently met with international visitors to the university.

Work in Athens had some additional personal benefits to me. After all my years on regional campuses, I enjoyed being back on a large campus. Performing arts events, athletic events, and even simply walking around campus were great fun for me. My colleagues at the executive level were talented and generous in sharing their expertise, and I enjoyed working closely with the presidents I served, Robert Glidden and Roderick McDavis. I maintained strong relationships with the provosts who were at the university during my years of service, and I'd like to think that I was a solid partner for them, as well.

On the whole, I enjoyed serving as vice president, although it was a demanding job. The hours were long, including both formal responsibilities and all of the more social or "ceremonial" aspects. There were more constituents or stakeholders to please and, therefore, inevitably more criticism to endure. There was a great deal of travel, although I enjoyed most of it. The physical distance of the campuses, however, sometimes made it difficult to anticipate issues or to quickly recognize concerns.

I am grateful for the fascinating career arc I had with regional campuses, from faculty member, to associate dean, to dean, and to vice president. I made a better living than I ever expected and had plenty of challenges to see what I could achieve. Not bad for a guy who just kept saying "yes" to opportunities, without any preconceived career plan.

2 Characteristics of Branch Campuses

OHIO UNIVERSITY ESTABLISHED ITS FIRST branch campuses in 1946, in Chillicothe, Portsmouth, and Zanesville. Classes met in the evening, in local high schools, and the purpose was to serve returning World War II servicemen. The intention was to provide general education classes, reducing the burden on the Athens (main) campus. The branches were expected to close once the high student demand had been met.

Instead of closing, however, the branches continued offering courses in response to local demand for the first two years of a college education. Students were expected to move to the main campus to complete their degrees, but the branches at least reduced costs and the length of time for which students would need to relocate. Both older and younger students could be served, and they were. When the branches opened their own buildings in the mid-1960s, on their own land, the university's commitment to branches became permanent.

A similar story could be told about other university branches in Ohio. All were created to serve as feeders to their respective main campuses, although baccalaureate degrees in elementary education were added at most, beginning in the early 1970s. Over the years, other baccalaureates were added at many campuses, and some served as sites for the delivery of selected graduate programs. Interestingly, some also offered technical associate degrees, if no technical or community college was located nearby.

It is worth noting that the development of this "feeder" type of branch in Ohio almost certainly was motivated by a desire to block the spread of community colleges. University leaders feared that community colleges could cut into a budget pie that was, as always, limited. That preemptive effort certainly failed. Community colleges have done well in Ohio, although there has been a long-running struggle between university branches and technical colleges, especially in seven communities where the two types of institutions are co-located.

The story in other states is often quite different. To my knowledge, Ohio, Pennsylvania, South Carolina, and Connecticut all created branches that were intended to focus on the first two years of a university education. In most other states, university branches were intended to provide local access to upper-division courses and graduate programs. In other words, the mission was just the opposite of Ohio's, intended to complement the work of community colleges, which provided the lower-division opportunity.

Community colleges also create branches, for reasons similar to those that motivate universities: to build enrollment and revenue, respond to some political imperative, or block an incursion by some other institution. Given the traditional mission of community colleges, however, main and branch campuses have essentially the same mission. My impression is that community colleges also have been quicker than universities to offer courses at various non-campus sites, such as high schools and businesses, but I have no data to support that point. What I do know to be true is that there are community college branch campuses with quite large enrollment (say, more than three thousand students), which is unusual, although not unheard of, for university branches.

There are many variations on the branch campus theme, and attempts to capture defining characteristics of branches have been challenging. Recently, the National Association of Branch Campus Administrators (NABCA) compiled a list of branch campus–related terms, and the results are more or less consistent with definitions that I've seen elsewhere. (The NABCA website, at www.nabca.net, provides access to some research and articles regarding branch campuses.)

According to the Commission on Institutions of Higher Education (CIHE), a branch campus is geographically removed from the main campus; offers 50 percent or more of an academic program leading to a degree, certificate, or other recognized credential; is permanent in nature; has its own faculty and administration; and has its own budgetary and hiring authority. The U.S. National Center for Education Statistics' Integrated Postsecondary Education Data System (IPEDS) defines a branch as a "campus or site of an educational institution that is not temporary, is located in a community beyond a reasonable commuting distance from its parent institution, and offers full programs of study, not just courses."

There are a handful of states that have coded the definition of branches into law, and other accreditation agencies have offered definitions. Florida, for example, recognizes three types of university branches, based on enrollment level and the range of programs offered. Nothing I've seen in state-level definitions deviates significantly from what I've described.

I think these definitions are good starting points. Offering a handful of courses in a shopping mall, at a high school, or in a place of business does not seem to create a branch. I'd call that a site. However, I'd also make a distinction between what I'd call a branch campus and an outreach center. The problem, as you'll discover quickly if you attend NABCA meetings, is that there are significant exceptions to any defining principle. Moreover, institutions do not consistently report statistics, or even addresses, for branch campuses and centers to national databases.

CREATING A PICTURE OF THE IDEALIZED BRANCH

As with so many topics in this book, if I want to expand on these broad definitions, I have little choice but to draw on my own experience and observations. There is something important at stake here, however. There is very little research on branch campuses that can help inform institutional leaders regarding best practices, or even common options. Therefore, I will offer a picture of what I consider to be the most common characteristics of the university branches with which I'm acquainted. I invite others to react to that description and, more important, to use it as a kind of benchmark, against which important variations can be identified and compared. I will point out some variations that I know to be important, but I cannot be comprehensive, because I do not know how to capture the variations in a systematic way.

So, is there anything to which we can point that will always be true about branches? I suppose there is an implication that there must be some "main" campus, hub, or mother ship in order for a branch to exist. Clearly, there is an implication that the branch is somehow in a dependent relationship to the central campus, at least concerning curriculum matters. Indeed, institutions in a true system, such as those in North Carolina, Wisconsin, or California, are not "branches," because they do have separate curricula and some independent governance processes, although such institutions can and do develop branches of their own.

From there, things get muddier, but let me share my own preferred descriptions of a branch campus and an outreach center. Think of these as idealized or prototypical descriptions, consistent with the CIHE or IPEDS definitions, but understand that individual entities will fit the description more or less closely. (Not ideal, from the perspective of people working on branches, but characteristic, in the sense of reflecting my own guess about what is most common.)

An existing institution establishes a branch campus in order to make higher education more readily accessible to people where they live and work. The branch has a permanent facility, usually freestanding, but sometimes shared. There is a local administration, providing a reasonably wide range of student services and support programs, although not the range one would see at the main campus. This idealized branch campus has a resident faculty, but curriculum control and the establishment of minimum faculty credentials come primarily from the main campus. I agree with CIHE and IPEDS that there must be geographic separation between the branch and main campuses, but I know the distance can range from just a few miles to hundreds of miles. Distance from the main campus does not seem to tell us much. My advice is to focus more on the administrative distinctions and decision-making authority. In the end, a branch is a branch because it lacks autonomy on curriculum and faculty matters.

What I call an outreach center looks a lot like a branch campus. The difference, to me, is that there probably are no resident faculty members and the programs and services are more limited.

I want to note that institutions sometimes create a campus to offer one specific program (e.g., marine biology) or to house a particular academic unit (e.g., a law school). Personally, I prefer not to refer to a location as a branch if it is offering exactly one program (say, a law school), and I expect that such a place does not think of itself as a branch, especially if it provides the only location for the program. I also struggle with calling a location that has no resident faculty a "campus." That probably reflects my own experience and my bias as a former branch campus faculty member. If there are resident faculty members, I have no problem referring to a university location as a branch if it happens to be located on, say, a community college campus, with or without a separate building.

If you accept my idealized concept of centers and campuses, you will find that many, perhaps most, institutions do not fit perfectly. The reality is that branches developed to meet particular needs of institutions or even state-level policy makers. No one regulated these developments, at least not in a thoughtful way, and no one was writing about the phenomenon, despite the remarkable expansion across the country and around the world. Jim Fonseca, until recently dean of the Ohio University Zanesville Campus, cowrote an article with me titled "Under the Radar: Branch Campuses Take Off" (Fonseca and Bird 2007), and I think "under the radar" is apt. While there are large numbers of students attending branch campuses and centers, and the number of such locations is expanding, it seems no one knows how they fit into broader higher education policy.

TWIGS AND TAKING EDUCATION TO THE PEOPLE

There are still other "definitional" matters to be considered. One of my own favorite topics is the emergence of twigs. Twigs are branches of branches. In most cases, I think a twig would tend to fit my notion of a center, rather than a campus, but the point is that they were created and are administered via the branch campus, rather than by the main campus. Again, I have no data, but my strong impression is that twigs, also, are expanding rapidly in number. I like the idea a lot. A twig has relatively low overhead expenses, but allows a blend of high touch and technology to support students and expand access.

Ohio University has three such twigs, which also meet my description of "centers." Of the two most established twigs, in my years of service, one is in Pickerington, Ohio, and is an extension of the Lancaster Campus. The other is in Proctorville, administered by the Southern Campus. In both cases there are a number of classrooms, including computer labs and interactive television classrooms. There is no resident faculty, but the university owns the buildings, and there is a modest support staff dedicated to ensuring that students and faculty members have a good experience.

The Pickerington Center demonstrates something interesting about the location of branch campuses and centers. Ohio University is located in the small city of Athens, and its branch campuses are in relatively small cities, as well. The Lancaster Campus created the Pickerington Center specifically to gain access to the Columbus metropolitan area, which has a population of more than two million people.

In other cases, urban universities are likely to open branches in the suburbs. Traffic, parking, concerns about safety (especially in the evening), and other elements of convenience mean that such universities can tap a student market they would be unlikely to reach from the main campus.

The most extreme example of this phenomenon I've seen was in Bangkok, Thailand. Traffic in Bangkok is unbelievable, and a distance learning provider with whom I met had ringed the city with classrooms and labs located in shopping malls. It was quite an operation, driven by the practicalities of transportation.

THE "PSYCHOLOGY" OF BRANCHES

I also want to mention some of the typical issues that emerge with branch campuses. As a psychology professor, I could suggest a definition of "branchness" that is based on the psychological characteristics of the people who work there. For example, nearly every branch person I've met has something of a chip on his or her shoulder. Branch folks feel unappreciated and undervalued by the main campus. They also feel that the main campus unreasonably, unfairly, and probably foolishly limits their development. In effect, people on branch campuses tend to feel suspended in a perpetual state of institutional adolescence, blocked from maturing into fully adult institutions. (Imagine how staff working at a twig must feel. They get a double dose of frustration, from their own branch campus as well as from the main campus.)

I spent twenty-three years on branch campuses, so I often share these frustrations. I also spent eight-plus years on the main campus, watching over five branches. From a main campus point of view, branches were created to accomplish some main campus purpose. The purpose may have been to generate revenue, to respond to some political pressure, to block some other institution's expansion, or even honestly to expand access and opportunity. But the core values of the institution developed, historically, at the main campus, not at the branches.

Thus, academic departments have legitimate concerns about standards or quality, as perceived by them. Budget and administrative support issues can further complicate the relationship. Not having direct oversight of the branches leads to worry about what is happening "out there." The natural, first response of main campus academic and administrative units is to keep the branches on a short leash, lest they "run amok." (I've actually heard people say those words: "We need to keep the campuses from running amok.")

For their part, the branch campus faculty and staff tend to feel that they should be allowed to serve their communities and students. They often feel that main campus personnel do not respect the professional judgment of branch campus faculty and staff and unfairly limit them. Hence, a significant issue to consider: To what extent does the branch campus have the obligation, right, and authority to meet the needs of its own community, if those needs conflict with the perceived mission and values of the main campus that created the branch?

Given these feelings, it is easy to understand why many branch campus personnel object to the term "main" campus. It seems to affirm the priority and authority against which the branch campus strains. Thus, we get terms like "mother ship," which is clever enough, I suppose. Personally, I actually prefer the term "main." To me, the dangerous ground for the branch campus is where its faculty and staff construct a version of reality that feels good but fails to recognize the political reality of their existence. Branch campuses succeed to the extent that they play the political game well. Getting to "yes" requires never forgetting who are on the other side of the table and how they view the world.

As a sidebar here, I want to mention that in Ohio and a few other states, many people also object to the term "branch." In particular, the main/branch distinction seems hurtful. Presidents often make a point of saying that they lead one institution, geographically dispersed. I appreciate the feelings and sensibilities involved, although I've never been personally bothered by the terms. Increasingly, I use the term "branch," only because it is the most readily recognized term around the country. Nevertheless, I may also refer to regional campuses or satellites, intending the various labels as synonyms.

SIZE AND PROGRAMS

A few more thoughts on what makes the idealized branch: I think size and programs matter. My own observation is that an entity with a student body of 700 or less has a hard time maintaining the number of faculty and range of courses and services that define the idealized branch. On the other end of the spectrum, as a campus grows beyond 3,500 students or so, it becomes necessary to subdivide faculty and departmentalize staff in ways that start moving away from the close collegiality and easy communication of a typical branch. I don't expect campuses with fewer than 700 students or more than 3,500 to say, "I guess we aren't a branch, after all." I'm just trying to get to an idealized notion, based on which we can think about variations.

I do think a researcher could usefully look at campuses or centers that are significantly smaller than my idealized campus. I know there are many locations that are considered to be more than a site, but that enroll only 100–200 students per term.

What are the particular issues of these institutions? What motivated their creation and maintains their operation?

Regarding programs, the question for me is the extent to which a campus has programs that are not available at the main campus. The idealized branch, I think, offers a selected range of main campus programs, or partial programs, that meet its specific market need. Sometimes, however, there is a need that cannot be met by an existing main campus program. For example, I mentioned earlier that some university branch campuses in Ohio offer technical associate degrees, because there is no community or technical college nearby to do so. Those degrees typically are not available on the main campus.

A few years ago, Ohio University created a baccalaureate degree, the Bachelor of Technical and Applied Studies, which is not offered at the main campus; and recently the university launched a Bachelor of Science in Applied Management. Both degrees are intended to articulate smoothly with technical associate degrees, from Ohio University's own branches or from community colleges, providing a baccalaureate completion option that meets the needs of adult learners seeking to advance their careers. Developing these degrees provoked considerable discussion, but in the end, proposals moved smoothly through the university's curriculum process. Similar programs, sometimes called the Bachelor of Applied Science or some other variation, are offered at other institutions.

These programs take us a bit away from the ideal. At some institutions, however, entire schools or colleges are located at a branch, along with other, more typically branch-type programs. For example, the University of South Florida has located a School of Hotel and Restaurant Management at its Sarasota-Manatee Campus. Given that there still is a range of other programs and courses, these campuses fit my definition of "branch," whereas George Mason's College of Law, located on a campus dedicated to that one program, would not.

Thinking of all this as a continuum, at some point of program expansion the result would be not branches, but a true multicampus system. I'm not sure where that point lies, but not surprisingly, I'd tend to emphasize how folks at the no-longer-so-main campus think about it, how the governance processes work, and whether the less-branch-like people view themselves as independent or an extension of a main campus. Accreditation could come into play, as well. For example, South Florida's Sarasota-Manatee Campus recently became accredited separately from its main campus.

This could go on and on. I hope my idea of the idealized branch makes some sense and that people may want to consider the implications of variation. It is not my intention to exclude from the branch campus tent anyone who wishes to belong. I merely want to focus on some core notions that can help organize thinking and discussion.

To summarize, then, my idealized branch is a permanent physical location, with at least some complete or nearly complete academic programs. There are some resident faculty members, and on-site services necessary to support faculty and students are available. There is a budget for this location, and day-to-day spending decisions are made locally. Fundamental academic control, however, is vested primarily in the main campus, which must approve any expansion of programs. Enrollment typically is between 700 and 3,500 students. Faculty members know each other and their students, and staff members typically wear more than one hat. Administrative offices are located close to one another, so that, from a student perspective, office boundaries are blurred.

AN AGENDA FOR BRANCH CAMPUS RESEARCH

As I mentioned above, my hope is that the idealized branch can be taken as a benchmark for studying the branch campus phenomenon. In the absence of a national database, we have to start somewhere. Graduate students in search of a thesis or dissertation topic, for example, could ask some interesting questions about the idealized campus, or they could compare branches with characteristics that vary sharply from my idealized branch campus and examine the implications. In fact, there is so little descriptive information available that even the most basic study could be useful.

I don't want to imply that there is no research at all on branches. Check out www.nabca.net, if you are interested, and click on the Resources button to find some examples. What bothers me is the lack of systematic study, not to mention a resource (other than nabca.net) to archive what has been done. I do want to add, however, that in the past few years NABCA's research committee has conducted some intriguing survey research that may speak to the same issues that concern me.

The core problem goes back to the fact that branches developed "under the radar," to meet some more or less local need. The decisions felt unique to the institution, or at least to the state. No one realized that this enormous chunk of the higher education industry was emerging nationwide and around the world.

So, as I've suggested, an urban institution may have opened a suburban branch to make attendance more convenient; a rural institution may have opened an inner-city branch to offer graduate programs to adult learners; a university may have opened a branch on a community college campus to facilitate degree completion. But if you go looking for best practices to help you establish your first branch campus, you will be sorely disappointed.

Thus, I would like to propose something of a research agenda, at least from a macro perspective that begins with the idealized campus. If I were going to pursue this research (and I'm not!), then I'd do the following:

FIRST, I would identify branches that fit my idealized model. I would distinguish between community college and university branches, but I would collect data on both. My description is brief enough that finding campuses that fit should not be too difficult, but it is important that they come from different states. I would not worry about other aspects of mission or operations just yet, because I want the first cut to capture campuses that vary quite a lot on other dimensions.

SECOND, having identified this study group, I would construct a survey to obtain descriptive information about how these campuses operate. What types of programs do they provide? What is the relationship of branch campus faculty to main campus departments? Where are decisions made about hiring and/or tenuring faculty? What is the title and authority of the branch campus's chief administrator? To whom does that administrator report? What services are provided? How is the budget determined and what is managed locally vs. at the main campus? All of these items could be teased out to create checklists against which any branch campus could be compared. In the end, we could have an expanded description of the idealized branch, including typical variations within the model.

FINALLY, although it may reflect my own discipline, I would probably try to do some more qualitative study on these campuses, seeking information about faculty and administrative perceptions toward the main campus, toward the formal mission, and toward career development issues.

The goal of this approach is to restrict the range of branch campuses being studied to those that are consistent with my "idealized" description, in order to get a handle on typical variations within the study set. Having accomplished the goal, research can proceed in many directions. For example, one could study the idealized campuses more deeply, drilling into, say, the role and relationships of faculty members, or examining mission or geographic differences to determine what effects they may have on enrollment.

An obvious alternative is to use the idealized branches as a comparison group and to begin studying campuses that do not fit the description. Suppose everything is true of a set of branches, except that there is no full-time resident faculty. What follows? Can we get at least a sense of the value or the cost of maintaining a resident faculty?

What if enrollment is well below 700? Am I correct in my assumption that it will be difficult to offer the needed range of courses and services, or not? What if most of the characteristics are in place, but the campus occupies a floor or two in a different institution's building? How does that affect the sense of identity for faculty, staff, and students at the branch?

In the end, we might have a decent description of major types of branches, which future scholars and campus leaders could use to ask questions that can be meaningfully examined. We might find clear best practices, based on some criterion, such as enrollment growth, or we might find a good description of start-up issues. I do believe more and better research on branch campuses could help inform important decisions going forward, given how the competitive environment and the impact of technology may change the role of branches. We need to understand more clearly how branches fit into the changing higher education world.

3 Politics, Purpose, and Practice

I WAS DELIGHTED TO STUMBLE ACROSS AN interview with Novice Fawcett, who was president of Ohio State when its four regional campuses were created (Fawcett 1984). President Fawcett told a story that is broadly consistent with what I know about the founding of Ohio University's campuses from reading various memos, interviews, and trustees' meeting minutes. But his perspective, especially with respect to Ohio University, is quite different.

Fawcett explained that university leaders had agreed to open branches to serve returning World War II service members, with the expectation that the branches would close when the need had passed. However, according to Fawcett, by the mid-1950s, only Ohio University had reneged on a deal among the state universities and continued to operate its branches.

Moreover, according to Fawcett, Ohio University was engaging in conversations with high schools to create additional evening branches, including one that would have been only three miles from Ohio State's Columbus campus. He felt that Ohio State should not "permit other state institutions, of what I thought were of lower academic quality than ours, to encroach on us in that manner." Later, after describing the process Ohio

State followed to open its branch campuses, he said: "This began to block off the Ohio University spread over the state."

Although I enjoyed reading the comments, I would challenge President Fawcett regarding academic quality, at least for most undergraduate students at Ohio University. I am also skeptical that Ohio University would have opened branches across the entire state at that time.

There is another little twist on the story. If you are into trivia about branch campuses (and who isn't?), here's an item: What university branch campus is closest to Ohio State Columbus? The answer is Ohio University–Lancaster, where I served as campus dean for four years after leaving Ohio State. In Lancaster, I was told that Ohio University agreed to create a physical campus (not in the high school) only when the leadership became aware that Ohio State was considering opening a branch there. I believe the story, but the fun is in imagining the presidents trying to outmaneuver each other to protect their turf.

THE POLITICS OF BRANCH CREATION

Clearly, one of the reasons universities create branch campuses is to block the expansion of competing institutions. In the days before interactive television and online courses, institutions' only means of reaching out was through the creation of branch campuses, centers, or sites. In a sense, branches were the "technology" that allowed for expansion.

Several years ago, I had an opportunity to write about the history of outreach programming at Ohio University, and I was fascinated by the story (Bird 2003). In 1914, the university hired three faculty members who rode trains and streetcars to deliver courses in towns across the region. In 1924, Ohio became the only institution in the state to offer paper-based correspondence courses, using the US mail for communication. Thus, branches were a natural progression, President Fawcett notwithstanding, when demand could support the cost of hiring faculty and staff, as well as operating and maintaining a physical plant.

There is every reason to believe that the university was sincere about expanding access in a rural part of the state, although there also is no question that there was interest in the tuition and state support that the campuses brought in. Providing extra compensation to faculty members for teaching these courses also helped address the problem of low base salaries, back in the 1940s and '50s.

I know of a few cases in which branches were created out of sheer political insistence from a state legislature. There is an interesting story about the opening of a university center in Tulsa, Oklahoma, that was intended to offer courses from several institutions. For a variety of reasons, the center was unsuccessful, leading eventually to the establishment of a rapidly growing branch of Northeastern State University, in nearby Broken Arrow, and expansion of Oklahoma State University, in Tulsa. Unfortunately, however, a previously thriving branch of Langston University, a historically black institution, found the going tough as the other institutions expanded offerings and facilities. Politics were definitely at work in that situation.

In another example of political force, a branch of the University of West Florida, in Panama City, was stripped away and given to Florida State University because a powerful legislator became impatient with West Florida's unwillingness to expand programs. Similarly, Ohio University lost its Portsmouth branch when an influential legislator insisted that it become a comprehensive four-year campus and the university refused. (Shawnee State University was the eventual result.)

The same things happen between community colleges. For example, I've seen commissioners from rural counties in Ohio push hard to get a community college branch in their county, believing that it would help attract employers and jobs to the area. I've sat in meetings, listening to administrators debate who would serve the county best and how facility costs could be handled, because (in the opinion of administrators) there was no way the county's population could generate enough enrollment to justify a campus.

I suspect that the major political concern, other than currying favor with powerful people, lies in competition for scarce resources. I'll have more to say about budgets and branch finance in a later chapter, but it is easy enough to appreciate that there never is enough state funding to satisfy the perceived needs of universities and community colleges. Adding campuses, whether branches or entirely new institutions, can mean smaller slices of the financial pie for existing campuses. From a more entrepreneurial perspective, if an institution can attract a larger share of the student market through its branch campuses, it might gain revenue at the expense of its competitors.

LEVERAGING THE POLITICAL
ADVANTAGE OF BRANCHES

Presidents typically do recognize that there are political advantages to having branch campuses. Ohio University Athens is in the district of one state representative and one state senator. However, taking into account the regional campuses, at least six representatives and four senators have an Ohio University presence in their districts. That's very close to becoming a caucus!

Moreover, branches typically have local community advisory groups, and if they are well selected, the university may have a set of influential leaders who can significantly leverage the political clout of the university's board of trustees, as well as support fund raising from an audience that otherwise might not be supporters of the institution.

Some years ago, there was a move at the Ohio Board of Regents to turn all the university branches into community colleges. Regents' staff built a strong case for the change, although it was not especially persuasive to the universities. The proposal had some momentum, until the various universities around the state engaged with their advisory councils to contact legislators. With twenty-four branch campuses across the state, legislators quickly got the message, and the idea lost traction, morphed into a set of "service expectations" for branches, and then quietly faded out of existence.

At the time of this event, I was associate dean at Ohio State Mansfield, and I had an opportunity to speak briefly at one of the public hearings that were held on the issue of transforming branches. My assigned topic was the economic development value of having a university campus in a community. My comment, just one of many on a variety of topics, was picked up statewide by newspapers and seemed to resonate with a lot of people.

For me, it was an early lesson that different constituencies have different concerns. Building community support for the branch presence may be mostly about jobs and economic development, whereas enrollment may be more a matter of providing convenient and affordable access for students. Internally, the political issues may be quite different, and campus leaders need to be engaged with all of the stakeholders.

BRANCHES AS COLONIES

Regardless of the internal reasons for founding a particular branch campus, such campuses exist only when there is a coming together of institutional interests and community desires. Typically, communities take real pride in "the branch," and over time their leaders will advocate for a broader mission and expanded programs. It is likely that the branch campus faculty and administration also will seek to expand mission and programs. Unfortunately, however, I can almost guarantee that the main campus faculty will resist that expansion and attempt to hold the branch to whatever its original mission may have been.

In my experience, there always are tensions between branch and main campuses. People at the main campus may doubt that the branch campus faculty and staff will adequately maintain whatever main campus folks believe they are about. (Usually, the message heard on the branch campus is that the branch falls short on quality or on breadth of course offerings. Sometimes it ties to arguments that all students should have a residential experience, which most branch campuses cannot provide.)

Main campus faculty members and deans may worry that the branch will compete with the main campus for enrollment, especially undermining enrollment in marginal courses and programs. I've never seen any evidence of this type of competition, and I've studied a great deal of enrollment data looking for it. Branches tend to serve different markets than the main campus serves, with more emphasis on adult learners and part-time students, in addition to attracting students who would not or could not relocate to the main campus.

I do see evidence that online courses compete with face-to-face courses for enrollment, but that is a different story, and the nature of the threat of online offerings to traditional enrollment is something institutions would do well to understand. For present purposes, I will simply note that a wise president or provost will manage online opportunities at an institutional level and not let branch and main campus faculties compete with versions of online courses.

Regardless, it has always struck me as absurd to expect branch campuses to be content with a very limited mission, and communities have every right to advocate for programs that meet their needs. Although I am no expert on colonies and colonization, I suspect that some insights into main campus–branch campus relations could be gained by considering the relationship between an established nation and the colonies it attempts to control at a distance. My own reading on the relationship between eighteenth-century England and the American colonies leads me to wonder whether that situation has similarities to the relationship between a university and its branch campuses. Maybe someone more knowledgeable in this area can judge whether or not the analogy has value.

If people at the main campus view their branches as colonies, then they probably feel a proprietary interest in the branch campuses, especially from an academic and financial point of view. Most likely, main campus faculty and staff feel that they have a right to oversee who teaches what on the branches; to limit programing; to direct student services; and to charge branches for services, for use of "its" courses, and so on.

(I couldn't begin to count the number of times I've heard a main campus faculty member say something about how his or her department "owns" the courses or the major. Frankly, I don't accept that statement, even for the main campus. If anyone "owns" courses and programs, it is the institution or the faculty as a whole, not individuals.)

I'm quite sure that many branch campus personnel feel like unappreciated colonists. Hal Dengerink, the late chancellor of Washington State University Vancouver, once said to me that branch campus faculty and staff need to understand that they aren't the "main thing," from the point of view of institutional leaders. That fact has a significant impact on effective institutional political strategy. Too much boat rocking may well produce unpleasant results for the branches, given that the branches were originally created to help solve a main campus problem, not to cause new ones.

I'd also expect the perspective of branch campus "colonists" to change over time. Early employees on a new branch campus often describe a sense of being pioneers, off in the academic wilderness, depending on one another for support, and engaged in the holy work of creating new access to higher education. Assuming enrollment grows and staffing increases, expansion of programs will seem logical to students, faculty and staff, and community leaders. It will not seem so logical to people at the main campus, who will tend to maintain perceptions (stereotypes) about the branches as originally created.

Still another potential issue relates to predictable conflicts over scarce resources. When money is tight, one can predict that the main campus faculty and staff will be concerned about any real or perceived drain of "their" resources. If main campus people perceive competition for students or dollars, they will almost certainly move to restrain branch campus growth. (I have heard lots of stories on that score!)

A colleague who formerly served at the University of South Florida's Sarasota-Manatee Campus, Peter French, has correctly observed on many occasions that if there is turmoil on the main campus, it will affect the branches, even if there is no mean-spirited intent. Political battles can lead combatants to court branch campus support, to attempt to deny the branch campuses participation in important decisions, or to use the branches as examples of the institution's "problems."

What happens if a branch campus grows to the point that it wants independence? I have no personal experience with a campus going its own way, so I don't know what struggles occur, if any. There are examples around the country of one-time branches that became freestanding institutions (e.g., Coastal Carolina University was once a branch of the University of South Carolina), as well as examples of relatively typical branches that gained a measure of self-determination (perhaps housing a school or college of the university, or pursuing separate accreditation and reporting lines to the president or trustees).

It isn't surprising that individuals associated with branch campuses would change their perspective over time. Especially if a branch was established a generation or more ago, that campus is by now the center of the academic world for its faculty, staff, and students. Local program needs and the opportunity for the professional growth of its faculty and staff are important.

Limitations that seem unnecessary or even disrespectful will produce resentment in branch campus faculty and staff. Over time, the local perception of mission is likely to grow somewhat distant from the main campus's original intention, and the branch campus folks may bristle at the "uninformed" or biased perceptions at the main campus.

Then again, my experience has shown that branch faculty and staff members underestimate their dependence on the support of the main campus, including the value of its "brand." In their frustration, they will sometimes push the boundaries, break the rules, or (much like an adolescent challenging parental authority) try to sneak courses, or even an entire academic program, past the main campus authorities. That may look like running amok to someone on the main campus and reinforce his or her biases. It might look more like the Boston Tea Party on the branch! (To be clear, I do understand that there are very serious issues that occur with colonization that are quite different from the relatively narrow aspects I am wondering about.)

What can be done to allow for the natural maturation of branch campuses, without somehow losing the essence of what the main campus feels the institution as a whole should be about? I suppose that is what many of us try to determine every day. I wonder if there are lessons from colonialism that could inform our thinking or, to be more scholarly, could lead to predictions about main campus–branch campus dynamics and evolution?

BRANCH CAMPUS STRUCTURES AND MISSIONS

Whatever else may come into play in the creation of a branch campus, nothing will be more significant to its future development than the initial decisions about structure and mission. By "mission," I am not referring to what some committee wrote on paper, but rather how stakeholders across the institution understand the mission (the *purpose*) of branch campuses.

When branches are created, decisions are made about what programs will be offered and how faculty members will be appointed. What will the financial relationship between the branches and the main campus look like? What sort of facilities will be provided? Which decisions will be made locally and which centrally? To what extent will the branches focus on community relations and the educational needs of the communities in which they are located? What student services will be provided?

The initial decisions set parameters that forever affect how the campuses develop. They set the boundaries for argument and to a large extent determine where points of tension will emerge. I will address program and faculty matters, as well as community engagement, in this chapter. I will consider financial, facility, and student service issues later. Others may well point to additional issues they consider important, but these are the ones that have occupied my time and energy.

FIRST CHOICES

I asserted above that branches exist when the interests of an institution come together with community desires. Although institutions increasingly pursue enrollment and revenue wherever they see opportunity, what I'd consider to be a "true" (idealized) branch involves an investment in facilities and faculty, so there are likely to be community advocates who urge and support that investment.

There is no shortage of communities clamoring for their very own campus. Even the political pressure to create branches likely stems from community pressure on elected officials or officials trying to ingratiate themselves with voters. Importantly, however, the success of a branch campus depends on offering those academic programs and services that the community can support. No matter how noble the institutional commitment to expand access and opportunity, branches that cannot generate the revenue to cover expenses will find it difficult to survive.

At the most basic level, the first choice to be made is the extent to which the branch mission will be the same as or different than that of the main campus. Dengerink (2001) discussed this issue and described how the University of Washington and Washington State University chose different directions. The former created branches with an assumption that their mission would differ from that of the main campus and that they would develop over time in different ways. Washington State, however, followed the path of "one university geographically dispersed," expecting all campuses to share the same essential mission.

In Washington, as in many states, university branches were limited (until some recent exceptions) to offering upper division and graduate courses, whereas community colleges provided the first two years of coursework. Because branches in Ohio were established to serve as two-year feeders, there always has been a difference between main campus and branch campus missions. Exactly how different, however, depends to a large extent on the nature of faculty appointments.

FACULTY APPOINTMENTS

Limiting myself to the two institutions I know best, I can state definitively that early decisions by Ohio State and Ohio University put them on different tracks. Indeed, I still feel some amazement at how different the cultures of the branches are at the two institutions, despite the fact that most of the campuses are of relatively similar size and operate as branches of public research universities in the same state.

To a degree, Dengerink's description applies to Ohio State and Ohio. Ohio State made more of an effort to tie the branch culture to that of the broader institution. Frankly, however, I don't think that was done on purpose. Rather, it happened more or less naturally, because Ohio State chose to think of its branch faculty as members of their academic departments. And, although there is general acceptance that branch faculty will not produce as much research as main campus faculty, very significant weight is placed on scholarship and publication. Branch faculty can and do serve on departmental committees, may occasionally teach graduate courses at the main campus, and are often members of the graduate faculty.

At Ohio, the situation has always been different. Faculty members are hired by the branch campus and tenured to that specific campus. Reversing the Ohio State process, main campus departments are consulted, but the vote is taken at the branch campus and passes from the campus dean to the provost. Academic departments do control teaching clearances on the branches, so there is a de facto veto, at least at the point of hire.

As an institution, Ohio University places more emphasis on undergraduate programs than does Ohio State, at least in terms of the relative amount of undergraduate instruction provided by full-time faculty. Nevertheless, Ohio is a research university, with significant graduate programs. That said, however, the expectation for scholarship was modest for branch faculty, especially prior to my appointment, in 1999.

Two observations underscore the cultural differences. First, Ohio branch campus faculty members teach heavier loads than those at Ohio State. Although calculated differently, the current load for most Ohio State faculty is two courses per term, whereas Ohio faculty members typically teach four. Yet, I think a quick survey would show that Ohio faculty members also teach an average of one or two overload courses per year, on top of that. (Overload teaching is relatively rare at Ohio State, outside of Education.)

The second observation is that as dean and vice president, at Ohio, I had a number of conversations with department chairs who told me that they had never met their branch faculty. Generally this happened when a student complaint made its way to the chair's attention or when we were asking for an upper-division teaching clearance, and the chair wanted documentation of the individual's competence to teach the course. In contrast, at least in my experience at Ohio State, our chair met twice a year with regional faculty, specifically to discuss our concerns, and most of us had regular contact with colleagues, especially in our own specialty areas.

I know there are exceptions to this description, at both institutions, but I am convinced that the cultural ties between branches and main campus are closer at Ohio State than at Ohio, and the connection is driven primarily by the nature of faculty appointments and the resulting expectations. Put another way, branch faculty at Ohio State tend to identify first with their disciplinary unit, and then with the campus. At Ohio University, it is the other way around.

PROGRAM DECISIONS

Another important mission-related issue lies in what we might call "mission conflict." In Ohio, the mission conflict is apparent: Branches are open access, with a strong undergraduate teaching mission. Scholarship is welcome and encouraged on the part of branch faculty, but expectations are below those of the main campus. Even after years of mission expansion, faculty members teach a *lot* of lower-division courses.

In Washington, I'm sure there are conflicts over which courses and programs will be offered, and the specifics may differ at Washington State and the University of Washington, but the mission conflict should be less than in Ohio. My guess is that people still debate whether a particular program will be offered at a branch, and if so, main campus colleagues say things about quality that are offensive to the branch faculty members. Nevertheless, there should be no debate over the qualifications of branch campus faculty members to teach a senior course to majors in their own discipline.

I can only assume that community college branches avoid the mission conflict issue, other than in terms of the debate over offering particular programs. I do know that there are issues with the proportion of adjuncts teaching on different campuses, which is drawing the attention of accreditors. I also know that many community college branch leaders feel frustrations that are similar to those of leaders at university branches, but the mission of providing the first two years of a baccalaureate education (not to mention complete technical certificates and associate degrees) must be the same.

Pulling this together, I maintain that regardless of what is written in mission statements, the mission-as-practiced will be driven by the relationship of faculty members to academic departments, and by decisions about program level or range. These two elements have a profound effect on how both main campus and branch campus faculty members perceive the branch mission. To this, I would append an additional defining element: how the branch and institutional leaders understand the significance of community engagement and partnership.

PARTNERING

Again, branch creation typically will include a story of community advocacy and commitment. No doubt, community leaders see the economic value that comes with having an institution of higher learning nearby. That presence will have limited impact, however, if the courses, programs, and services offered do not address community needs.

Unfortunately, universities, and especially research universities, tend to be inwardly focused. I will restrain myself from a full-out rant here, but even when research universities propose partnerships, they rarely understand what it means to create an *engaged* partnership. An example that involved an Ohio University college and a nearby community college may illustrate what I mean:

A few years ago, the dean of one of our professional colleges approached me about arranging a conversation with several community colleges, to explore creating articulation agreements. I was pleased, but also surprised, because the college had always before been a reluctant partner.

Enrollments had declined in the college, however, and reduced state support had forced the university leadership to tie budgets more closely to student credit hour production. The dean knew that my staff had built strong relationships with community colleges, so it made sense to ask us to initiate a conversation.

We arranged the meetings, and the assistant dean of the college accompanied my staff to the community college. As soon as everyone was introduced and took their seats, the assistant dean spoke up, saying, "We would like to create an articulation agreement between our programs and your institution. I reviewed your curriculum and prepared curriculum sheets to show how your program articulates with ours. You'll see that students cannot reach the baccalaureate in just two years, but if you make the changes I've indicated to your existing curriculum, the fit will be better."

The community college dean asked a few questions about course scheduling at the university, given that most of her graduates were working full time and would need to commute to the university branch for some courses, and to the main campus for certain courses and labs. She wondered about online options or the possibility of offering some courses on the community college campus. She also asked for more detail about course transfer, hoping to find a few more matches than the curriculum sheet showed.

The assistant dean patiently explained that there was no way around lab requirements, and there were no facilities available other than at the main campus for certain critical lab experiences. Faculty members, he explained, are pressed by their research expectations, so travel to the community college was not possible, in most cases. He did express willingness to consider offering labs on Saturdays, but he couldn't commit.

So the articulation agreement was created and signed, but there was virtually no increase in transfer enrollment. Those of us involved in outreach (branch campus and distance learning staff) were frustrated at the failure to use this opportunity to build another bridge. The difference between what the assistant dean viewed as "partnering" and what we considered to be an engaged partnership was critical.

When universities come to listen, community colleges feel respected and valued as colleagues. University representatives need to demonstrate some willingness to examine assumptions about curriculum and about serving new student audiences. When community college representatives come to listen, they get a better understanding of legitimate concerns that the university leadership feels, so that the university does not appear simply to be rigid or arrogant.

In an engaged partnership, institutions have the potential to design curriculum and develop services that support student success. Because their relationship grows over time, the institutions might create entirely new programs or degree options never before considered. They might engage in co-marketing, dual admissions, and shared advising. They surely will identify hurdles and overcome them, increasing the likelihood that community college students will naturally select the partnering university to continue their education.

These partnerships are happening, and for universities, it does make a difference in attracting enrollment. But engaged partnerships require deep listening and willingness to seek common ground, in creative ways that yield high-quality programs, while adjusting to the legitimate expectations of our students.

In fairness, my thinking about community engagement has evolved over the years. As a faculty member I was primarily concerned about my own career and the performance of my students. However, as I became more involved in public speaking and community service, my sense of the role a campus could play began to change. I served on the local mental health board while still a faculty member, and a colleague talked me into joining the Rotary Club. The people I met in Rotary literally destroyed my assumptions about leaders in the business and professional community. On the mental health board, I first discovered that I could make difficult decisions that were driven by mission and priorities, and I relearned the importance of giving back, after years of too much self-absorption.

My growing sense of community responsibility became even stronger when I served as a campus dean. Lancaster, Ohio, had experienced an economic turnaround after its major employer was sold to a larger company. When I arrived at the campus, I was impressed to see how many local leaders praised the campus (and its previous dean, Ray Wilkes) for not only responding to requests for involvement but also taking a powerful leadership role, bringing people together for dialog, listening to new ideas, and designing effective programs that made a difference, especially in the area of workforce development.

That said, I was frustrated by how often there was a perceived need, on my campus or in the community, to which we were not able to respond. Typically, it was an issue tied to an unresponsive academic unit at the main campus but sometimes it was simply a matter of the institution responding far too slowly or lacking a legitimate program or set of courses for whatever the purpose might be.

Moreover, there have been frustrations when someone expected the universities to respond in ways that either didn't make sense (e.g., a plant manager who wanted Ohio State to offer a bachelor's degree in welding—not welding engineering, but *welding*) or had no potential to generate enough enrollments to sustain the requested program.

All colleges and universities should be open to new ways of partnering, and a sensible approach would be to involve more than one institution, when appropriate. Although main campuses occasionally collaborate to offer joint programs, the whole nature of truly engaging with a local host community, and its institutions and employers, is not well understood. Branches could lead the way with this type of engagement, but for that to happen, the main campus needs to encourage and empower branches to do so.

GOING DEEPER: WHY BRANCHES MATTER

At least for someone like me, who has invested much of his career in branch campuses, the purpose of branches also has a strong emotional element. These campuses matter, and far too many people, both on main campuses and branch campuses, fail to understand adequately why many branches thrive and how they make a difference. As a result, institutions may not fully exploit the strategic potential of branches. Even if the primary interest of the main campus is to use branches as a cash cow, it behooves leaders to understand what works and what does not.

Some of the strategic importance of branches should be obvious. They offer access to higher education, usually with flexible scheduling and relatively small classes. Most branch campus instructors are highly committed to teaching, ahead of whatever scholarly interests they may maintain. Staff tend to wear multiple hats and to work in physical proximity to each other, so administrative departments do not have the sense of separateness that one finds in more highly departmentalized situations—with the result that students are less likely to be passed from one office to another.

Learning support may not always be what we'd like it to be on the branches, but compared to many main campuses, at least at large research universities, students perceive a high level of caring. Faculty members tend to be available to students and willing to discuss academic concerns. In part because of the inherently interdisciplinary character of branch campuses, faculty members may be more likely to discuss concerns about students with each other and to recognize problems in time to support a student's success. (As always, my perspective is tied to my experience with branches of research universities. The distinctions may be less apparent at community colleges or at teaching-focused universities.)

The cost of attending a branch campus may be considerably less than the cost of attending a residential campus. In Ohio, tuition on university branch campuses is typically lower than on the main campus, but this isn't true in all states or at all types of branches. However, even for students of traditional college age, families tend not to consider the cost of providing room and board at home in the overall cost of attending college. Students at branch campuses may accumulate less in loans and can actually work their way through school, a near impossibility at a residential main campus.

All of this represents generalizations that are commonly true but not universal. If you believe as strongly as I do in the potential of branch campuses to change lives, then you'll also be disappointed when you encounter a cynical or unengaged faculty or staff member or an administrator who doesn't seem to embrace the mission. Moreover, I found the main campus commitment to undergraduate education at Ohio University to be sincere and strong. I can argue that branch campus students do not receive a lesser educational experience than main campus students, but not that they receive a superior experience.

The real drama of branch campuses, in my opinion, lies in the personal stories told by their students. Sure, some students attend a branch because they lack the motivation to do anything else. However, I've seen audiences reduced to tears by students telling stories about how their lives were turned around because of access to the education provided by the local branch campus. These powerful stories can serve an institution's leadership well if they are used to illustrate not only how the institution is engaged with employers and communities but also how the institution achieves the goals of trustees and state-level policy makers.

On top of the political value described earlier, at Ohio University we found that our branch campuses have access to donors who are not necessarily alumni and would never donate to the main campus, so there are opportunities for gifts that are unlikely to be otherwise obtained. Broadly speaking, the community engagement and local access provided by branches build support for the institution that can be helpful and demonstrate the value of the broader institution. (To illustrate, the five Ohio University branches raised more than $20 million in the University's Bicentennial Campaign, the first in which the branches participated.)

Finally, those who are familiar with the book *Good to Great* by Jim Collins (2001) will recall that he makes an important distinction between foxes and hedgehogs. Foxes look great and run around doing many different things. Hedgehogs, which may be less attractive, do only one thing, but do it exceptionally well. Branches tend to be hedgehogs, at least as compared to main campuses. That is, they may lack the status of the main campus, but, at their best, they are very focused on a mission of access and service. The result is that many branches pursue their local markets with clarity of purpose. Main campus leaders could benefit from considering how and why their branches succeed or fail.

Keeping human and financial resources focused often produces stronger financial results, as well, which may serve broader purposes of the institution. In fact, I'd argue that part of determining whether a branch campus is needed should be demonstrating that it can fully cover its costs and help support institutional priorities. In my opinion, it is fundamental that demonstrating need implies demonstrating enrollment and net revenue that make the good investment obvious.

Branch campuses, then, serve a variety of purposes for institutions, including the noble commitments we all celebrate. The purposes served may not be a high priority to everyone on the faculty or in the administration, but the leadership definitely ought to get it. Well-placed and well-supported branch campuses can become one of the most valuable assets of a higher education institution.

4 Students

OFFERING PEOPLE THE CHANCE TO WIN A single relatively big prize in a lottery can motivate more people to enter than offering many small prizes or incentives. Accordingly, when I was at Ohio State Mansfield, as an incentive to attend an evening information program for adults interested in coming to college we held a drawing to award some lucky person a free class.

The drawing was a nice touch and worked well. Another element of our program was that we had several current adult students attend and talk about their experience at the campus. Although it can be a little scary for an administrator to give students the microphone, I've found that it is an important part of this type of event. Students may say things in ways that sound awkward to faculty and staff, but it is easy to see prospective students responding to people like them who have had a good experience at the campus.

I always kicked off the evening's program and then went to the back to listen to students and members of our staff speak. One evening, after we had held our lottery for a few years, I heard one of the most stunning and effective student presentations ever.

A senior student I'll call Jane got up and talked about how scared she was to come back to school. She described all the usual fears: could she succeed academically; would her family be okay; would she fit in? Jane decided to attend our evening program and see what she could learn, but even that was frightening to her. She drove to the campus and parked, but sat in her car crying.

Jane was a religious person, so she prayed that God would give her a sign, if going back to college was the right thing for her to do. Then, she dried her tears and left the car. I'm sure any reader can see what was coming: When we held the drawing for a free course, she won! As Jane said, that seemed like a pretty clear sign, so she took the one course, and four years later, she was about to graduate with a degree in education.

We couldn't have planned a better presentation, as Jane talked about her success, how faculty and staff members encouraged her, and how comfortable she was at the campus. Honestly, I was stunned, but the marketer in me was thrilled. Believe or don't believe in God's plan, but that night it felt like He was watching over the Mansfield Campus—or, maybe better, He was leveraging Jane's experience to connect to additional adult learners.

BRANCH STUDENT CHARACTERISTICS

Students choose to enroll at a branch campus for a reason. Adult learners may have different reasons than younger students, but there also is a great deal of overlap.

Research on adult learners consistently shows that older students place the highest value on the program they want, offered flexibly and at a good price (see Harms 2010). From experience, I would add that institutions with first-rate support services that are of relevance to adult learners have a better chance of retaining students when they encounter obstacles to their continued enrollment.

I remember a woman who was a single parent with four children. She worked part-time and consistently made the dean's list while carrying a full-time course load. Like many adult students, she was pursuing a dream and was forced to be extremely well organized and focused, which no doubt contributed to her ability to do well under difficult circumstances.

I've known many adult learners who needed a bachelor's degree in order to advance in their current careers, as well as many others who wanted a degree that would support their move into a new field. Overwhelmingly, and regardless of how much they may have enjoyed school, adult learners enrolled in order to create a better life for themselves and for their families.

Still, there were many other stories. I had a student who enrolled because her husband told her she was boring. And when she realized that she wasn't boring at all, she divorced the husband. I knew an English major who had more than 100 credit hours over the requirements to graduate, and when I asked her what was going on, she said she loved learning and wanted to take every course that interested her before taking the last requirement in English. (Today, that would raise questions about state support, but at the time she was married to a guy who supported her learning addiction.)

I had a terrific student who was a farmer and came to school every Winter Quarter, just because he enjoyed learning and wanted a degree. Winter was the only time he had enough freedom to attend class. (Today, I imagine he might enroll in an online or hybrid program, but there were no such options back then.)

Many adult learners are examples of what psychologists call the Zeigarnik Effect—a sort of drive to complete an unfinished task. Still, most adult learners are purpose driven, and that purpose is tied to jobs and quality of life for their families.

The story is more varied for younger students. Years ago, I had eighteen-year-olds in class because their parents didn't see any point in their going to college and wouldn't pay for them to attend.

I haven't heard that in a long time, but especially with a grant or loan, it remains possible for students to work their way through college at a branch campus, if they continue to live at home.

Finances play a part in the decisions of more and more young students, but usually there are other elements, as well. There is both an academic and a social adjustment that comes with leaving home to go to school, and some students (or their parents) see an advantage in starting at a community college or at a feeder branch before leaving home. Of course, many students are not academically ready to leave home, and many of the students at Ohio State and Ohio University branches were not admitted at the main campus. Nevertheless, I think a careful study of the motivation of young people to attend a feeder branch or to transfer to an upper-division branch after community college would show that they prefer the smaller campus and believe they will get more personal attention from faculty and staff.

Keep in mind that although students may start at a branch of the Ohio type or at a community college because it is cheaper than going away to school, in every case I know, the diploma received with a baccalaureate degree says nothing about where a student attended the first two years. Starting at a commuter institution is a perfectly legitimate way to get an education *and* a residential experience, without incurring the cost of four years away. One interesting implication is that "feeders" should be seeing more strong first-year students (e.g., with higher ACT or SAT scores), and that is at least true at Ohio University. It was true at Ohio State, when I was there, and I assume it continues to be the case.

Less positively, I have often heard students give as the reason they are at the branch, "My dad said he isn't paying for me to attend the main campus when I don't know what I want to study." Even worse: "My grades last semester weren't very good, so my mom said I had to come home and attend the branch until I do better." Gotta love the idea of the branch as a punishment for undecided or struggling students. You can imagine how pleased faculty members are to hear that they are the booby prize.

So, we can expect students to choose branches because they are less expensive, but we also know that many students prefer smaller campuses. I've seen many examples of students putting together a class schedule that includes classes on two or three branch campuses, in order to avoid attending the main campus. Sometimes this is an issue of distance; sometimes it is tied to perceptions of safety or parking, if the main campus is urban and the branches are located in relatively rural areas.

Frankly, students give other reasons for avoiding the main campus that one hears with regularity. There are reports of professors who make nasty comments about branch students or the branch professors, and branch students often report that they feel faculty and staff members at the branch care more or are more available to them. Students who have experienced small classes and gotten to know their instructors outside of class are unlikely to be pleased by large lecture classes or TAs who are less qualified to teach than their branch professors.

My limited experience with upper-division/graduate branches suggests to me that there are many similarities. However, by definition, their students have succeeded at another institution before transferring, so one would expect a high retention and graduation rate. Moreover, all of the two-year "feeder" type of university branches I know of now offer baccalaureate completion programs, either independently or through partnership with other institutions, so the distinction may be less clear than it once was.

STUDENT SERVICES

Branch campuses tend to pride themselves on their engagement with and support of students. In my experience, however, too many times branch staffing is so lean that students struggle to get access in a timely way. Keep in mind that most branch students, regardless of their age, commute to campus, juggling school with part-time or full-time jobs; and many have some sort of family responsibility, if not other claims on their time.

When I see a campus that closes its student services office from 12:00 until 1:00, it makes me angry. We all need a lunch break, but the traditional lunch hour may also be the time when some students need to call or visit. Closing at 5:00 for the day is problematic for the same reasons, but the worst thing I've seen is offices closing at, say, 4:00, so that staff can complete paperwork before leaving for the day.

The latter example is common on main campuses, and if a main campus office serves branch students (e.g., a financial aid office or bursar's office), it creates still more problems. I raise the same caution for institutions that hope to attract more adult learners to the main campus. Having consulted with a number of such institutions, I can tell you that attracting adult learners requires thinking about their needs, not expecting them to conform to yours.

I emphasize this because I am stunned by how often institutions continue old practices that assume students will adjust to the practices of the institution, instead of engaging with students to develop a deep understanding of their needs. In this highly competitive age, in which students have many options for pursuing their goals, being insensitive about service is a serious mistake.

To emphasize this point, I often argue that student support services, from the point of inquiry to graduation, are the critical differentiator for prospective students. If a thirty-year-old working adult with a family decides to return to school to complete a degree, he or she may be considering online options, commuting to a main campus, or attending the local branch. Because adult learners value flexibility, price, and time required to earn the degree more than brand, and because they almost certainly have multiple options for whatever degree program they want, it is a buyer's market today.

To illustrate, in the early days of personal computers, on-campus computer labs represented an important service. Many students did not have access to a computer at home that had enough computing power to meet their needs. Even today, a surprising number of people are using old equipment or connecting through a dial-up modem, with the result that branch campuses may be the last to phase out these labs. (This also can be a problem for online programs, especially if they are serving students from rural areas.)

Back in the day, we created a nice lab at Ohio State Mansfield, and it was open well into the evening, Monday through Friday. A few students approached us to complain that the lab was closed on the weekend. Crowded lab conditions during the day, and family responsibilities at night, were keeping them from getting on a computer during the lab's established hours. After surveying students for the hours that would be most helpful, we wound up creating Sunday afternoon hours and found the usage at that time more than justified the expense of being open.

There are other similar examples of understanding branch student needs. For example, young students living at home with even younger siblings may find it difficult to study, creating a need for open hours at the library that have little to do with direct library service, but everything to do with student support. I applaud the move to create a "learning commons" that serves multiple needs for group projects, quiet study space, and access to computers, as well as staff support for those with questions.

For all this, branches will continue to have a lean staff. I offer a special plea to be data oriented in developing and providing services. For whatever reason, support units often fail to collect even basic usage data that would inform staffing decisions, hours of operation, and the like.

It is so important to let services be data driven. Otherwise, you not only may fail to provide a needed service but also may create inefficiencies by responding to perceived needs that have no real impact. I can't count the number of times I've had a faculty member or a student tell me about a grave need for a particular service, based on talking with one or two students. Being the experimental psychologist I am, I looked for data to support the argument, and it just wasn't there. I've also allowed services to be piloted, if the start-up costs weren't too great, to see whether or not the service was of value. Sometimes it was, and sometimes it wasn't.

Lean branch staffing reinforces this need for data. For example, at very small branches, with two hundred students or fewer, I have seen situations where there were no resident faculty and only two or three staff members, including the campus director. (Note that I would call this location a center, not a campus, but the distinction is immaterial for the current purpose.)

If the director makes a pitch to add a position, the pitch will be most effective if it is tied to helping with recruitment or retention. Providing data to support the argument and describing the proposal as a pilot project is often helpful. ("Pilot" is a magic word. I've gotten away with many things by calling them pilots, when I anticipated that the new service would be permanent.)

STUDENT LIFE

Branch campuses commonly struggle to provide much in the way of student life programs. Their students are commuters, probably with at least part-time jobs, often enrolled less that full time, and frequently with family responsibilities in the evenings.

Early in my administrative career, I was frustrated to discover that many of our young students would not attend an on-campus event on Friday evenings in the fall, because they were going to their former high school's football game. At the time, I shared the belief that student life is a critical component of an effective retention program. I still believe that can be true for some younger, especially full-time, students, but I doubt that it is a major concern for others.

At both Ohio State Mansfield and Ohio University Lancaster, we worked hard to create connections with our students outside the classroom. Some things worked reasonably well. For example, in Mansfield, we had a very active psychology club. (I think it still is doing well.) However, I remember struggling with the feeling that students should lead the club, and a faculty member should stick to being an advisor.

The problem was that, even on a campus where the psychology major was popular, some years we had strong student leaders and some years we did not. If the faculty members didn't step up in a "down" year, to make sure the club stayed active, it could lose its momentum and be lost.

My point is that, even when a student organization is established, on a branch campus student leadership development can be a challenge. To some extent, I'd suggest just going with the flow. I can think of at least three or four occasions when students wanted to create a student newspaper. In each case, we agreed to support the project, and in each case the paper survived for less than two years. Nevertheless, as long as they had an advisor and worked within a budget we could provide, I was happy to support the effort.

A particular concern is student government. Again, students have approached me at different times to create a government, and I always was agreeable. I've seen branches, especially those with somewhat larger enrollment, maintain a consistent student government from year to year. At my campuses, however, that never happened during my years of service.

When I was chair of the Faculty Assembly at Mansfield, the campus dean was concerned that the lack of any consistent student voice could be an accreditation issue. He and I worked together to create a student advisory board for the dean, with members nominated by the faculty. That solution seemed to work well. We could make sure the body was appointed from year to year, we had a process that made membership something of an honor, and we had members who were bright and thoughtful. At Lancaster, we also did not have student government, and I tried to replicate the Mansfield solution, but with less success. At Lancaster, however, the associate dean helped establish a chapter of a two-year student honor society, and we were able to use that group in an advisory capacity.

Enjoying sports as I do, and believing that it is important to encourage physical activity, I always was a supporter of strong intramural programs. My campuses had physical activity centers, but I've known of others that took advantage of off-campus venues. In Ohio, there actually is a university branch campus athletic conference. From a main campus perspective, the teams are clubs, but the last I knew, there were seven or more sports, and the student athletes loved the opportunity to compete. Only a subset of the twenty-four campuses across the state are involved, but the cost is very modest.

Engaging adult learners in anything like a traditional student life program is especially difficult. Clubs oriented toward the major can be attractive, and just in terms of creating some spirit, we found that weekend picnics that included the whole family were popular.

Despite these examples, there are three general points I'd like to make about student life on branch campuses. First, to the extent that the purpose is to see students engaged in meaningful activities outside of class and to develop leadership skills, at branch campuses it may not be necessary for the institution to provide the opportunity. Students are living in the community that has been their home, so some may be involved as volunteers at local nonprofits, whereas others may be active in their churches, in politics, or in organizations that support their children.

Second, I've often felt that branch campus staff members have unrealistic expectations for participation. Consider the ratios: If a main campus has, say, 10,000 students, and a club has 50 members, a branch campus with only 1,000 students would meet the same level of success with only 5 participants. Now, it may or may not be worth the effort to serve small numbers of students, but the difference in scale is something to keep in mind.

Finally, there are excellent opportunities to include service-learning components in many classes. Through service learning, instructors can encourage community engagement and accomplish many of the goals of student life programs.

I continue to believe that student life can be an important element of the branch campus experience, especially at campuses with a substantial daytime program that serves a significant number of full-time students. But the challenge is great, and the approaches may need to be modified in line with the differences in mission and in student population.

COURSE SCHEDULING

As I learned more about university branch campuses outside Ohio, I discovered that course scheduling is often an overwhelming challenge. Frankly, I was stunned to discover that many branch campuses have little or no control over the courses offered, the days and times chosen, or the instructors assigned. In multiple cases, the branch administration was not even told when a class section was added or cancelled. It amazes me that those branches do as well as they do! My own experience with scheduling, by contrast, was very positive.

In my first few years as the associate dean in Mansfield, my responsibilities included developing the schedule of classes, as well as finding adjunct instructors and working with main campus departments, when coordination was necessary. At least for a while, I found schedule building to be an interesting puzzle.

I was fortunate that the campus dean established some boundary conditions that helped control the potential for chaos, such as insisting that daytime classes meet only for one hour, between 8:00 and 2:00, with a few exceptions. We also agreed with the faculty leadership that all full-time faculty members were expected to teach at least one evening section. (At Lancaster, where the evening program was significantly larger than in Mansfield, many faculty members had an evening class every term.)

The insistence on one-hour classes was significant, at least in our case, because it helped immeasurably with potential course conflicts. Importantly, it allowed me to go to our full-time faculty and simply ask them for their preferred teaching schedule. I had been advised by several people that asking faculty members for their preferences would cause all sorts of problems, but that did not prove to be the case.

Given our boundary conditions, it turned out that we had faculty members who liked to teach early in the day, and some who preferred teaching in the evening. I took the faculty requests and laid out the schedule by general education category. I also had data indicating which courses students tended to take together, and recommendations from our academic advisors about courses that at-risk students should *not* take in the same term. In addition, I asked our English and math faculty to caucus and give me their recommendations, and I *always* let the Education faculty develop their own schedule. (In my experience, colleges of education seem to be continually in a state of curriculum revision, meaning that they have multiple programs operating at the same time. In addition, various field-based methods courses needed to be coordinated carefully.)

I could go on, but the point is that we were able to build a rational schedule that minimized conflicts and met the great majority of full-time faculty preferences. I also met with evening students on a quarterly basis to hear their concerns and ideas.

Those meetings were very helpful in crafting an evening schedule that was efficient and cost effective.

The campus dean challenged me to build a two-year schedule, so that students and advisors could plan effectively. This was important, because some courses were offered only once a year, and a few were offered only every other year. I actually built a three-year schedule, to adequately capture the course rotations. I built a four-year evening schedule, although without days and times, for the same reason.

I became a student of course scheduling, and I learned a lot. In a sense, I was fortunate, because campus enrollment was near a low point in our traditional cycle of between about 1,050 and 1,200 headcount, when I started. We had significant budget issues, which also raised the urgency to build a cost-effective schedule.

(The measure I point to for cost effectiveness is average section size. On a branch campus it often is important to let sections go forward with only a few students enrolled, either to complete a sequence or to help students complete their program, but average section size remains a good indicator of how well the overall schedule works.)

As enrollment grew, we added classes. Sometimes, it was helpful to create additional sections of already-offered courses, especially if they were required. Sometimes, I could add different courses to expand general education options. Moreover, by having a multiyear schedule, I could remove some sections and increase the average enrollment per section, while actually improving course access for students. I collected data on student satisfaction with the schedule, and it went up from year to year with our approach.

I still had some main-campus-driven frustrations. At Ohio State, for example, to teach Intermediate Accounting, even an adjunct had to have a master's degree in accounting and a CPA. An MBA/CPA wouldn't do, and qualified folks aren't easy to find! In addition, the emphasis on scholarship meant that we had very little overload teaching, and we rarely employed main campus faculty, with the important exception of the College of Education. At Ohio University, many faculty members taught overload, including faculty members from the main campus. However, their desire to earn the overload salary with the least inconvenience sometimes created scheduling challenges.

At Ohio State, more than at Ohio University, our orientation toward enrollment data also documented a lack of demand for courses at certain times of the day. For example, we had a couple of faculty members who wanted to teach required classes from 3:00 to 5:00, two days a week, to get around the dean's rule on one-hour classes or to minimize competition from more popular classes. However, at least in Mansfield, those were hours that neither day nor evening students would accept, so we offered very few classes at that time.

In Lancaster, we were offering three foreign languages (Spanish, French, and German). Because we offered the first quarter of each language only in the fall, enrollment tended to decline steadily, from term to term, with the result that we lacked sufficient enrollment to offer the second-year sections. When I suggested we cut back to two languages, some faculty members were unhappy, until I pointed out that it might be better actually to provide the full two years of two languages than only one year of three. We tried it, and it worked out well.

In the next chapter, I will have more to say about thriving as a faculty member on a branch campus. Here I mention only that as an associate dean I supported faculty members offering the occasional course that we knew would enroll only a handful of students, if it happened to be more closely related to their research interests or to some other passion. A strong class schedule can accommodate that practice without compromising efficiency.

Finally, as much as I believe that scheduling can and should be data driven, all data are inherently retrospective. I always was open to the occasional "experiment" to see whether a new course had potential. Of course, we evaluated the results before offering the course again.

I have gone into detail to emphasize that branch campus scheduling can be based in readily available data, and that a truly student-centered class schedule can be cost effective. What won't work is the approach too many campuses take: either letting faculty members decide when they will teach, without some boundaries and relevant data considered; or letting main campus department chairs decide what will be taught at the branches and at what times, based on their own interests rather than on the needs of the branch campus.

This problem is further aggravated if the instructional budget is in the office of the main campus dean or the main campus department chair. In those cases, it is absurd to expect the dean or chair to place branch needs ahead of those on the main campus. I will say more about branch campus funding and the power of good revenue-sharing models in a later chapter.

I will close here with a word of advice to presidents and provosts: It is absolutely poor leadership to say that you want to see enrollment grow at your branch campuses (or in your online programs) and then allow decisions that require knowledge of the local community and branch students to be made at the main campus. The main campus does *not* know best when it comes to recruiting and serving branch campus audiences that, by definition, are different from the audience on your main campus.

Frankly, the same is true for main campus–based programs for adult learners and for online programs. These programs should be student focused and not an attempt to generate additional enrollment without understanding the "market." For the great majority of institutions, your brand will not be strong enough to compete if your programs, scheduling, and services are not in line with student needs. Embrace the hedgehog, if you want to thrive.

5 Branch Campus Faculty Members

IT SHOULD BE APPARENT FROM MY PERSONAL story, outlined in chapter 1, that I feel grateful for whatever forces led me to serve as a faculty member at Ohio State Mansfield. It was a good fit for me, in many ways, although I couldn't have known that at the time of my interview and hiring.

Nevertheless, writing about branch campus faculty members may well be the most difficult challenge in a book that is continually challenged to capture the range of regional and branch campus structures and experiences. I believe that decisions about faculty appointments are the most important factor driving branch culture, both for good and for ill. They have extraordinary impact on branch governance, on student experience, and on main campus perceptions.

Describing the role and influence of faculty is further complicated by the scarcity of research on which I can draw. Moreover, in my own experience no two campuses have been alike. I don't mean that they varied in some minor details; I mean that they have been quite distinct. Because my direct service was limited to two public research universities, I recognize that drawing conclusions from my observations on visits to other institutions is vulnerable to my personal frames and biases.

The behavior of faculty members on branches also is affected by whatever sense of the branches as colonies exists on the main campus. As the branch campus faculty matures, especially if most are on the tenure track, they tend to have the same attitudes as main campus faculty: They expect to run their own affairs, and they resent anyone who tries to control them, including main campus colleagues in their own discipline who may determine what courses they can teach, and when.

Further complicating the situation, there are university branches with tenured faculty members, and there are branches where no faculty members are on the tenure track. Some branches have a few resident faculty members but rely on the main campus or adjuncts for most teaching; and some branches have a relatively large resident faculty, supported by local adjuncts, but with very little instruction provided from the main campus. Many branches do their own hiring and course scheduling, with varying levels of involvement from the main campus; but at others, all faculty members are accountable only to the main campus academic units, with course schedules set by the chairs of those units, sometimes with little or no input from the branch campus leadership.

As a reminder, although my idealized branch includes the presence of resident faculty, it does not specify exactly how faculty members connect to the branch and to main campus departments. Even internally, relatively large branches may have a departmental or, more likely, a divisional structure for their faculty, whereas smaller branches may work more with the faculty as a whole. Of course, when branches have few, if any, full-time faculty in residence, quite different questions and concerns emerge. Even regional accreditors can affect the status of a branch, if they become concerned about different patterns of instruction at branches, centers, or off-campus sites.

MY OHIO STATE AND OHIO UNIVERSITY STORIES

To flesh out these issues a bit, I will start by describing my experience at Ohio State and Ohio University. Then, I will add a more general description of my observations about institutions that either do not distinguish between branch and main campus faculty roles or do not appoint branch faculty on the tenure track at all.

At Ohio State branches the first generation of faculty members included many Columbus campus doctoral students, hired at the instructor rank. Most remained master's qualified (ABD, perhaps), without any strong expectation for research. Teaching at the lower-division level, their assignments were more consistent with Columbus teaching assistants' than with tenure-track faculty's. As a result, whether fairly or unfairly, Columbus faculty did not perceive the branch faculty members as peers.

On the other hand, from the beginning, Ohio State's branch faculty members held "no salary" appointments in their academic departments. Indeed, the story is told that seven years or so after the founding of regional campuses, someone in Columbus realized that, under university policy, all of those initially appointed branch faculty members were tenured, by virtue of their years of service. At that point, most were promoted from instructor to assistant professor, and they remained in that rank for however long they continued to serve.

The university leadership realized that the branches had become a permanent part of the institution (which was not President Fawcett's original vision), so departments were required to develop promotion and tenure guidelines for branch/regional faculty members. In most cases, that meant a significant expectation for research and scholarship. For the first generation of faculty members, this led to a sense that they were not respected or valued, and some became bitter about new research expectations that they could not achieve and had not anticipated when they took the jobs.

Nevertheless, beginning in the early 1970s, faculty members were hired with PhDs, through national searches, and they entered as assistant professors. When it came time for decisions regarding tenure and promotion, the primary vote took place in the academic department, with the case proceeding to the relevant college dean. In my years at Ohio State, I never saw anyone achieve tenure over the objections of the branch campus faculty and dean, but I saw a number of individuals who were supported by the campus turned down in the department or college office, always on the issue of research productivity.

As a result of the emerging research expectations, which many of us considered to be an opportunity, not a threat, Ohio State began to attract and retain a strong branch campus faculty, in the most traditional sense. (That is mostly, but not entirely, a compliment to Ohio State, as will become clear below.)

I was hired in 1976, and as a faculty member in psychology, I participated in psychology department meetings, conducted some of my research on the main campus, became a member of the graduate faculty, served on master's committees, and was mentored/supported by main campus colleagues. I achieved tenure and promotion in the department, with a good record of research and publication, and then participated in votes on hiring and tenure, regardless of the campus on which the position was based. No one would have confused my research record with that of a faculty star, but as one senior colleague put it, I was "on the stage," having a number of articles in top-tier journals.

I don't say this to brag, but to emphasize that there was a culture at Ohio State that strongly linked faculty members to their disciplines, with an expectation that branch faculty members might produce a smaller quantity of publication, but that the quality should be high. For humanities professors that typically meant publishing a book before the tenure decision. For those of us in scientific fields, it meant having a reasonable number of articles in solid journals.

At Ohio University, the situation was and is quite different. Branch campus faculty members are hired and tenured by the campus, not by the academic department or even by the branch campus system as a whole. The academic department does have input and controls clearances to teach specific courses, and it is consulted on promotion and tenure decisions, but the decisions are made at the campus level and sent forward to be reviewed by a committee of branch faculty members, before going to the provost.

Note that branch campus faculty members are most definitely not considered to be members of the main campus academic department. Some departments take a sincere interest in their branch faculty, and on occasion a branch faculty member might be included on a departmental curriculum committee. However, it is common for faculty members on branch campuses not to learn about curriculum changes, for example, until they have been implemented.

When I first came to Ohio University, I was surprised to learn that faculty members often were encouraged to teach overload courses. I understand that overload contracts yield low-cost instruction, because instructors are paid at levels close to those for adjuncts. However, the implication was that Ohio University faculty members were teaching considerably more than their counterparts at Ohio State.

The truth is that many Ohio University branch campus faculty members were carrying teaching loads, including overloads, that looked more like the loads at community colleges than at research universities. Because this practice existed for years, some faculty members relied on overload and summer teaching to maintain their lifestyles. As a result, there was little, if any, time available for traditional scholarly activities.

Practices changed somewhat after I became vice president. Within our ability to do so, we discouraged consistent overload teaching, not only through what we said but also by encouraging more thoughtful course scheduling and by hiring additional faculty. With direction from the provost, we ended the previous practice of awarding tenure without promotion, and we made clear that we expected faculty members to be positively engaged in their disciplines. The expectation for "positive engagement" included an expectation that there would be some evidence of peer-reviewed publication to support a case for tenure.

I received a lot of pushback over some of these changes. Not being totally naive, I tried to be consistent in my language on each topic, but not rigid on specific cases. I was serious about the idea of positive engagement. It remains my belief that the best faculty members genuinely love their disciplines, and they demonstrate that by continuing to learn and explore. If they are good at what they do, they should occasionally have discoveries that are worth sharing, through conference presentations or publications.

On the other hand, I did not believe that Ohio University's faculty could or should have expectations that rose to the Ohio State level. Our teaching loads were higher, even without additional overload. In addition, we specifically encouraged the scholarship of teaching and engagement, as well as more traditional work, which was not typical at Ohio State, at least when I was there. Moreover, I remembered well how that first generation of faculty members felt at Ohio State, when the research expectations increased, and I had no interest in beating up on our "founding" fathers and mothers. Again, I realized that we sought a long-term cultural change, so that the greatest emphasis was on the newer faculty members.

I was motivated, in large part, not only by my personal values and beliefs but by the charge I was given to strengthen the academic reputation of the branch campus faculty. To support this effort, we added a variety of programs and other support for faculty scholarship, but we also strengthened our promotion and tenure review processes, and we involved academic departments more directly in our hiring process.

I believe we successfully implemented the changes we sought, but it was definitely a challenge. To this day, I believe that Ohio University comes closer to the notion of best practice on branch or regional campuses, but my own heart and natural reactions tie more closely to the practices at Ohio State. Honestly, for me, it comes down to how we perceive branch missions, and it will always be thus.

OTHER APPROACHES — EXAMPLE 1

As I've suggested, there are many different approaches to the appointment of faculty members. One of my most positive consulting experiences was an eight-month relationship with a strong regional university that is primarily committed to teaching and service. Faculty members are expected to be active scholars, but even on the main campus the expectations are modest by the standards of a research university. Moreover, the president actively encouraged the scholarship of engagement and teaching, something I believe more presidents should do.

There was a collective bargaining agreement at this institution, which drove many decisions that affected faculty. Although faculty members were appointed either to the main campus or to their only branch, there was no formal distinction in mission, and both teaching loads and salaries were the same. Indeed, faculty members occasionally moved from one location to the other, and cross-campus *on-load* teaching was much more common than at Ohio State or Ohio University.

I was impressed by what I saw. Because mission and expectations were similar, there was little or none of the mission conflict that arises at some institutions. As usual, some academic units were more positive about the branch campus than others, and there was grumbling at the branch about unreasonable limitations, but I also saw genuine academic leadership coming from the branch, and I heard much less stereotyping between the branch and the main campus than I've heard at most institutions.

In addition, distance can have a significant effect on inter-campus relations. At this institution, the campuses are only fifty miles apart, making travel back and forth relatively easy. Moreover, the branch campus was in a larger city, with the result that some main campus faculty members lived there, and there was the draw of shopping and the arts to encourage familiarity.

OTHER APPROACHES—EXAMPLE 2

I can illustrate the implications of mission and distance with another example. I visited a branch campus of a major research university that is located two hours from the main campus. This branch has an upper division/graduate mission, and enrollment has grown significantly over the years. The branch benefits from strong state-level political support, but main campus support, especially from academic units, is a long-standing issue.

The main campus places heavy emphasis on research, closer to the level of Ohio State than Ohio University. In recent years, main campus priorities became increasingly national in scope, and academic units moved even further from any emphasis on outreach and engagement, although I'm sure the institutional leadership would claim otherwise.

Some years ago, the branch campus began to hire its own faculty members, but it was not allowed to appoint anyone to the tenure track. This practice has caused significant frustration at the branch campus, and the branch leadership was further challenged by the lack of any financial incentive to main campus units either to provide instruction or to support branch campus growth and expansion. Frankly, without that strong external political support, I believe the branch campus would have been closed years ago.

Interestingly, although there are cross-campus tensions, the environment on the branch campus is largely positive and hopeful. All faculties have their issues and enjoy grumbling, but the relationship between faculty and local administration is as strong as I've seen.

Reasons for the positive atmosphere may lie in the nature of the mission of that branch campus, as well as in the fact that all faculty members were in the same non–tenure track boat. Many of the branch campus faculty members had spent considerable time in nonacademic careers, so they were pleased to be working at any university campus. Many had strong community ties and were well known off campus. For these individuals, the branch environment was an excellent fit, and expectations for their performance were fully consistent with a branch mission.

In a very positive move, and with support from the provost, the branch has been given considerable independence to develop and deliver programs that meet community needs. Struggles with main campus academic units continue, but the combination of distance and difference in mission is working well for the branch campus.

MORE OBSERVATIONS

Despite variability across institutions, I am struck by the similarity of faculty concerns. To be sure, there are strong cultural effects of mission, distance, and the form of faculty appointment. Both local and institutional leadership significantly affect growth and reputation. Nevertheless, many branch campus faculty members feel underappreciated, generally underpaid, and held back by colleagues at the main campus.

One major complaint I hear is that the main campus academic department fails to communicate with branch faculty or to include them in discussions that affect them directly. In many cases, faculty members have stories about being denied the opportunity to participate in what appear to be institution-wide programs for faculty development. They may feel unreasonably restricted in the courses they are allowed to teach; they tend to believe they carry excessive responsibilities for institutional service; and, if there are research expectations, they feel they lack time, the support of graduate students, and necessary facilities. There is truth in all this, but in fairness, it is a one-sided truth that is better informed about branch campus challenges than about workload and time pressures for main campus faculty members.

Additional challenges occur: In far too many cases, chairs and deans perceive time and energy spent on branch campus issues as an opportunity cost, distracting them from more important priorities. In some cases, chairs or deans express hostility toward branches, but in most cases they simply ignore them as much as possible. Branch leaders spend an inordinate amount of time helping newly appointed chairs and deans understand how branch campuses contribute to the institutional mission. In my opinion, the difficulty is aggravated if chairs and deans perceive no direct financial benefit to their academic unit from supporting branch enrollment.

Understandably, all this contributes to a sense of frustration for branch campus faculty members, not to mention administrators. They often feel that departments and colleges should invest more time in their branch faculty members, and that they should express more concern over their welfare.

Frankly, that isn't going to happen. The branch, by definition, is at a distance, and it is not the first priority for anyone on the main campus. Telling deans, chairs, or administrative department heads that they "ought" to take more interest is fine, but expecting it to happen consistently yields disappointment.

Building bridges requires that someone take initiative, and that initiative almost has to come from the branch campus. Indeed, this is one reason I generally favor having some central leader located on the main campus who thinks about branches every day. In the end, however, the most effective thing is for individual branch campus faculty members to develop strong relationships with their main campus academic units.

Intuitively, it seems to me that community colleges should not have these issues, since the mission and typical faculty credentials are relatively consistent across campuses. However, when I speak with community college branch campus faculty members, I hear all of these same complaints, including frustration created by the main campus blocking the addition of courses and programs at its branch campuses.

As a final comment, I also have visited a number of small branches that have fewer than half a dozen resident faculty members. Faculty members on these campuses have unique challenges, in part because they are spread so thin. Advising loads are very heavy, and everyone is expected to pitch in on recruiting. Nevertheless, both administrators and faculty members, for all their frustrations, consistently expressed a sense of adventure and commitment to students and to each other that I found inspiring. At these small branches, pursuing growth and development could generate additional revenue and help meet their most pressing needs, but too often there is no established revenue-sharing model to support investment. (More on that in the chapter on finance.)

SO HERE'S THE RUB

As I've suggested, it seems to me that whether these variations in faculty appointment work well or create difficulty depends on how they align with institutional mission. What, really, is the purpose of a branch campus? What courses and programs should be available, and how does an institution assure comparable quality? How are decisions about courses and programs made, and by whom?

At most institutions with branches, the diploma does not indicate which campus delivered the courses, so the "value proposition" begins with an assumption that the degree is equivalent—if not identical in all respects—regardless of where the courses were taken. Is that true?

In my opinion, we in higher education tend to look inward to define mission and to make claims of excellence. At Washington State and Ohio State, the decision was to minimize differences across campuses. So, they hire faculty members with PhDs, maintain comparable expectations for them to stay current in their fields, and assess their stature through the same departmental and college processes that are used on the main campus. They acknowledge that there are some differences, but the focus is on similarity.

At least at Ohio State, I believe this view of mission and faculty has served the institution well, but over my years as associate dean, I began to feel that we should be more engaged in meeting community needs, instead of more or less telling the community what we were willing to provide. At Ohio State, the same "one university" perspective Dengerink described at Washington State drove us. Although I grew up professionally in that culture, and I find it personally comfortable, it doesn't necessarily follow that this "one university" approach is in the best interest of communities or students.

Again, the question lies in how we think about mission. If branches exist to serve the needs of their students and communities, they should not necessarily look or act just like the main campus. Community engagement, for example, takes on a different quality. Appropriate faculty professional development may be different, with pedagogical research or the scholarship of engagement "counting" more than it might on the main campus, at least at institutions like Ohio State and Ohio University.

If branches exist principally to extend the reach of the main campus, then maybe everything should look as much like the main campus as possible, but what about the interests of other stakeholders (adult learners, employers, etc.)? I believe we were more responsive to community needs at Ohio University, although not in anything approaching the fully engaged way that I'd like to see. Sometimes the issue is openness on the part of main campus academic units, but often it is merely a matter of the needed program not existing at the institution, or of an employer perceiving a need for which there is simply not enough employment opportunity to support a program over time.

A BRIEF NOTE ON GRADUATE PROGRAMS

Graduate programs at branch campuses almost certainly are affected by the cultural relationship between branches and the main campus. In most situations, the target audience at branches is not future scholars and professors. Rather, the programs almost always support professional advancement for students. Thus, it is common to see the MBA or programs for teachers delivered, but it would be rare to see a graduate program in physics, unless it was a "physics for teachers" program or was tied specifically to the needs of a major employer.

At Ohio University, we offered a much more robust set of graduate programs on the branch campuses than Ohio State did, but very little of the instruction was provided by branch-located faculty members. That has changed a bit but essentially remains true: the campuses provide the location for delivery and some of the support services, but not the actual instruction. (In one significant departure, regional faculty members provide nearly all the instruction for a program in Communication, collaborating across campuses to cover courses. That's a nice model, except for the fact that the instruction is done on overload contracts.)

My impression is that circumstances are significantly different at branches where the mission is restricted to upper division and graduate programs, although the types of faculty appointments are as diverse as at other types of campuses. An interesting research project would be to explore the relationship between branch and main campus faculty members at institutions with a substantial branch campus graduate mission.

GENERALIZATIONS AND STEREOTYPES

For the most part, I enjoyed my relationships with faculty members, as individuals, and I lived comfortably in the world of shared governance. My interests are broad enough that I genuinely enjoy hearing about other people's research interests or their latest teaching experiment. I enjoy people with a sense of humor, even if it is relatively cynical, and there are many faculty members with a cynical sense of humor. In the end, if one understands the rules of the game, it shouldn't be impossible to get things done.

Overwhelmingly, faculty members work hard. With a handful of exceptions, people who thrive on a branch campus tend to care deeply about their students and to be willing to share the service load. The work-life balance can be better without certain of the pressures of the main campus, and for those who become involved in community service there can be a true sense of making a difference.

Personally, being a faculty member is central to my own professional self-concept. I'm proud of professional achievements that tie to my discipline, and I am especially proud to have achieved tenure in a department as distinguished as Ohio State's. There are many elements of being a faculty member that are almost in my DNA, with the result that I experience cognitive dissonance between what is natural and comfortable for me and what I believe is in the best interest of institutions and of the public.

An especially slippery topic, when it comes to the role of faculty, is the issue of shared governance. Given my own disciplinary background, I naturally assume it is a good idea to encourage participation in decision making by people who are affected by the decision. The problem comes when people not only expect to be kept informed and to have a voice but also expect that their individual views must rule.

There is nothing unique about regional campus faculty members in that regard. Some are collaborative, some are aggressive, and some just want to be left alone to do their own work. Administrators learn to roll with the differences and to be patient in reaching decisions. The slow progress of faculty governance, especially around curriculum, may become a bigger problem in the future, but except when I felt people behaved dishonestly, I never found governance issues to be especially stressful.

What did change for me, over the years, was my appreciation for the interests of other stakeholders, especially when there were implications for enrollment or budget. Serving as an associate dean made me much more aware of how students and support staff were affected by policies and decisions, whereas my years as an associate dean and campus dean heightened my appreciation for needs in the communities we served. As a vice president, I learned more about the political realities faced by institutions and the need to consider the perspectives of alumni, donors and political leaders in our decision-making.

SEEKING A SATISFYING CAREER

The only published study of branch campus faculty members of which I am aware is by Nickerson and Schaefer (2001). Through a national survey of branch campus chief administrators, they attempted to capture at least some elements of faculty life. Unfortunately, their data do not come from faculty members, but the results are consistent with my own impressions and experience.

According to Nickerson and Schaefer, branch campus faculty members enjoy teaching, appreciate the mission of outreach, and value their relative autonomy, which is sometimes described more negatively as allowing them to avoid main campus politics. The administrator-respondents report that their branch campus makes more use of adjuncts than does the main campus, and I would guess that is even truer more than a decade later. Respondents describe their faculty as younger and with a larger proportion of women than the main campus, but I suspect that is very campus-specific, depending on when the campus was founded.

I'm not especially comfortable trying to capture the typical life of a branch campus faculty member, but a few observations may be in order. For example, an individual faculty member may be the only representative of his or her discipline, with English and mathematics being the major common exceptions. Even if there is more than one faculty member, they likely have been chosen to cover different areas of specialization, so research collaboration is difficult.

Opportunities to grow professionally may be more limited on branch campuses. I taught seventy sections of general psychology before I moved to administration, and one reason I never wanted to go back was that I truly did not want to teach that course ever again. On the other hand, when I chose to retool, from experimental to industrial psychology, no one objected, and I found renewed energy. That energy didn't offset the fact that I didn't want to teach general psychology, but retooling opened all sorts of doors for me, both as a faculty member and as an administrator.

In my opinion, institutions would be well advised to consider thoughtfully how to support branch campus faculty members across a thirty-year career. Expecting them to be happy in what amounts to a perpetual stage of adolescence is unfair and unwise. Academic careers often have a sort of rhythm to them, and facilitating growth from, say, the tenth year to the twenty-fifth is in everyone's best interest. This may imply allowing the mission of the campus to evolve, as well, and that can be difficult to achieve.

One of the most rewarding aspects of being a branch campus faculty member can be the opportunity for almost daily cross-disciplinary interaction, which I believe is much more common than on main campuses. One of my best memories of the years in Mansfield is from the lunchroom, where it was common for a dozen or more faculty members to gather around the table. Sometimes people were simply relaxing, joking around, or sharing experiences. Sometimes we talked about more serious topics, and I recall one colleague saying that on almost any topic one could imagine, we had someone around the table with real expertise on the subject.

Two of my best friends were in history (one mostly American history and one more European, of course), and I learned a lot from them. I especially valued my colleagues in psychology, as individuals, but also for our shared core knowledge and vocabulary. Other good friends were in physics, biological sciences, English, and social sciences.

My experience as a branch campus faculty member was invaluable when I moved into administration. I had learned quite a bit about disciplinary differences in how scholarship is valued and how teaching approaches vary, not to mention where the hot buttons were likely to be on various issues.

Thinking back over the hundreds of faculty members I've known, and considering those who thrived and those who did not, as well as those whom I consider to have been strong contributors and those I do not, the happiest seemed to be those for whom the campus was a good match between their interests and those of the institution. There is nothing especially surprising about that, but it is worth emphasizing.

At Ohio State, I had a clear message to share with candidates: People do well here if they genuinely enjoy teaching undergraduates but also want to stay active as scholars. Those who just want to teach will struggle for tenure and for above-average salary increases. But those who feel shortchanged because they aren't directing doctoral dissertations, and those who deeply want research to be their primary activity, will be equally disappointed.

On the negative side, because of the nature of a branch campus faculty, dysfunctional behavior can be more damaging than might be the case on a main campus. For example, I remember a situation in Lancaster, where an individual was in constant conflict with students. He was perceived to be unpredictable, unengaged in the classroom, and disdainful. As a result, his department at the main campus had pulled some teaching clearances, and because he was the only person teaching in that discipline, quite a few students had to travel to a different campus to take a required course that he no longer taught.

I have little patience for faculty members who look down their noses at branch students. It is bad enough when a main campus faculty member is disrespectful and disengaged toward the branch and its students, but it is profoundly offensive when it is a member of the branch campus faculty itself. Such individuals exist, and it is frustrating to encounter that attitude.

Finally, I want to mention something that could become a growing issue in the years to come. Branch campuses can no longer rely on geographic location to protect their enrollment. With online and hybrid options, more competitors are emerging. The greatest threat, however, may turn out to be internal. As pressures increase on the main campus to maintain or increase enrollment while also addressing budget issues, I anticipate that some academic units will attempt to pull back what they allow their branches to offer. They may conclude that they can provide online options, instead of face-to-face courses, keeping the revenue for themselves. Leadership may also view branches as carrying expenses that can be eliminated via a "virtual campus."

This could become a golden age for branch campuses, but for that to happen, presidents and provosts must step up and insist on an institution-wide strategy to serve various student audiences. Emphasizing instruction for adult learners and other nontraditional students, and using hybrid delivery and the so-called "flipped classroom," branch campuses can continue to serve a regional audience and compete effectively with fully online alternatives. I will have more to say on this topic in the final chapter.

6 Branch Campus Support Staff

IF THERE IS A SINGLE LEADING REASON I stayed in administration instead of returning to the faculty, it was the opportunity to work with campus support staff. My enjoyment came as an unexpected surprise, and I'm sure it was affected by the fact that I was never lower than number two in the campus hierarchy (better to be boss than bossed), but my gratitude for co-workers runs deep.

When I became associate dean at Ohio State Mansfield, I had served on the faculty for more than ten years, and I had filled a number of faculty leadership roles. I knew all the staff, and I felt we had cordial, if not better than cordial, relationships. However, there is a world of difference between working with people on committees, or chatting with them in the hallways, and working with them every day in a hierarchical environment.

Before I moved into administration, I'm sure I believed that any motivated person could do administrative work, including student services; I'm sure I was skeptical about the value of graduate work in student affairs. I know I thought that administrators make too much money and have too much power in relation to the faculty.

My assumptions were quickly tested. In my new role, I was responsible for academic advising, among other things. Ohio State had made the decision years before to create a University College as the enrollment unit for most first-year students and to provide advising through a professional staff, rather than through the faculty. (Students still had faculty advisors in their major, but University College students were not officially admitted to their majors.) Branch campus advisors were considered to be University College advisors, although in our context they also worked with students who had been admitted to a degree-granting college. (I should mention that Ohio State eliminated University College sometime after I left the university.)

Over the years, I heard many complaints from students about the Mansfield academic advisors, and I occasionally felt the advisors were giving poor advice, especially as it related to psychology majors. As I considered personal goals for my time as acting associate dean, I thought that "fixing" the advising issues would be a worthwhile contribution. I felt that there could be no excuse for the "misinformation" our advisors had been giving students.

Now, years later, I feel foolish writing those words. My goal may have been to fix advising, but to my surprise, I learned that advising didn't need to be fixed, at least not in terms of the information provided to students. In close to 100 percent of the cases, when I followed up on some complaint from a faculty member or a student, the advisor had documentation at hand to show that she had given the student appropriate advice; the student in these cases either didn't follow through, "forgot," or flat out misrepresented the advice.

The issue, of course, was that all my information about advising had come from students who were upset or didn't like the advice they had received. I didn't hear from students who were pleased, and I didn't hear from the advisors at all.

My response was to do for the first time what I did many times thereafter. I developed a survey of student satisfaction with advising, as well as with other services that reported to me. The result was documentation that our advisors were doing a good job, along with some constructive ideas for how we could improve further. That's when I got lesson two: discovering that some of my faculty colleagues didn't believe the results, because they "knew better." I've always been amazed at the ability of some people to look right at the data and conclude that their own perceptions (biases?) are more correct.

I remember talking with my contact in University College and telling him about my "discovery" that our advisors were giving out good advice, but that students either seemed not to retain the information or failed to act on it. He laughed and suggested that I consider the freshmen and sophomores in my classroom. If average students score around 75 percent on exams, why would I expect those same students to remember 100 percent of what advisors told them? If students didn't follow my advice on how to do well in my courses, why would I expect them to do what advisors recommend?

Over the years I learned to respect and appreciate the experience and expertise of staff, in advising, admissions, finance, and other areas. In nearly all cases, they were dedicated, engaged, and concerned for student success.

Along the way, I also realized that working with staff was in many ways more congenial than working with faculty. Individual staff members don't always get along or cooperate to the extent we'd like, but they tend to start with an expectation of cooperation and an interest in finding solutions, instead of parsing ideas in search of their flaws. Moreover, if you happen to be their supervisor, their default option is to do what you ask them to do, at least after expressing their concerns. I liked being in charge, and I found that I was pretty good at delegation, a critical administrative skill!

Serving as associate dean was a great role for me, at the time. I enjoyed working with our faculty, and I'm proud that I remained friends with nearly all of them. Spending a large portion of my day with staff, however, was satisfying, and my appreciation for their abilities grew over time. After ten years in the classroom, the challenges of administration were fresh and energizing. I found that marketing was fascinating, with measurable results, so that became a strong interest for me. I enjoyed working with others to create strategies to grow enrollment and improve retention, and both financial and enrollment spreadsheets helped satisfy my need for occasional immersion in data.

A NOTE ON LABELS FOR STAFF

Institutions have different labels for employees in various categories. In my terms, "professional staff" refers to individuals who provide student and institutional support services. Most work on an annual contract; all or nearly all have at least a baccalaureate, but usually a graduate degree. I am not including individuals with specific academic administrative responsibilities, such as deans, chairs, or program directors; nor, for the most part, do I include campus executives.

Similarly, institutions refer to hourly employees in various ways. I will use the term "classified staff," which may be more common at public institutions, but I intend it to refer to individuals who provide office support and, in some cases, direct services to students or faculty members, or both. Most have more specific job descriptions than professional staff, and rules for evaluation and advancement tend to be more specific and less flexible. Staff working in buildings and grounds are classified, but I won't have much to say about them here.

WHAT SERVICES TO PROVIDE

Almost by definition, a branch campus does not provide the full range of programs and services found at the main campus. For example, varsity sports are located at the main campus, not divided among the main campus and its branches. (At least, I've never heard of an exception to this. More than one campus in a system can have varsity sports, but a system is different from a main campus with branches.) Indeed, the NCAA has rules that affect the ability of student athletes to enroll in branch courses, or so I've been told.

So, what services *should* be provided by a branch campus? The answer, certainly, depends on the campus mission, level of enrollment, and cost to provide the service. Part of the premise in creating branches is that they will be less costly to operate because the main campus can provide some services at little or no additional cost to the institution. In Ohio, acting on that premise has allowed university regional campuses to keep tuition significantly below that of the main campus. In some other states, the difference in cost is captured to benefit the general institution.

As a rule of thumb, I believe that those services directly affecting student recruitment and retention should either be provided on the branch campus or at least be accountable to the branch leadership. Precisely because there are differences in mission, programs, and student characteristics, those who are most knowledgeable should be in charge.

As a second rule of thumb, I believe that what I call "backroom" services, such as financial needs assessment, billing, and, usually, registrar functions, should be centralized at the main campus. Centralization of these services is more cost effective, more easily managed, and generally invisible to individual students.

RECRUITMENT

For the most part, marketing/recruitment, admissions counseling, and academic advising should be located at the branch. I've never seen a main campus admissions office do a good job of recruiting for branch campuses, for example, and if you believe you have an example where it works well, I suggest digging a little deeper, to make sure. That digging should go beyond asking your own staff or students, and should involve learning more about how other institutions approach recruiting.

We had a great approach to recruiting at Ohio State, because the level of trust was high between the main campus and the branches. Simply put, our Mansfield recruiters did all the high school visits and college nights in our service area. I think we sincerely believed that students who qualified for admission and wanted to attend the main campus should do so, and we also learned that being honest brokers served everyone's interests. Our staff's credibility with high school guidance counselors, for example, seemed to be very high.

In addition, we had an outstanding relationship with the local alumni chapter. The most active alumni at that time had not attended our campus, but they loved the Scarlet and Gray, and they were committed to seeing the branch campus thrive. The alumni sponsored an annual campus day for guidance counselors, at which we shared information that applied both to the main campus and to our campus. Local alumni also held an annual "Beat Michigan Bash," at which an auction raised funds for Mansfield scholarships; and they raised money to update our student services area, giving it a much more obvious Ohio State appearance.

I suspect that the main campus also "trusted" us because they knew full well that their recruiters and admissions staff could fill the main campus class quite nicely, no matter what we did. Thus, there was little or no concern that we would somehow take students from them.

Ohio University also had an effective, if less collaborative, approach. Branches did their own recruiting, but generally were not expected to recruit for the main campus. (Both campuses often attended the same high school college nights, for example.) However, again, relations were generally cordial.

Of course, financial aid is a big concern for branch campus students. Both Ohio State and Ohio University have financial aid staff on their branch campuses. In my opinion, financial aid information is complex and continually changing, so students are best served if they speak directly with a specialist for anything beyond the most general information. I believe there is value in cross-training, especially on branch campuses, but I think financial aid counseling is an exception.

Some financial aid support can be centralized at the main campus, but if enrollment is sufficient to justify the expense, I believe it is important to have financial aid counselors who are on site and well known to students. I've seen counseling provided from the main campus, but unless a person is assigned specific responsibility to serve branch students, such counseling rarely meets student expectations. Emotions run too high, and students today have too many other options for enrollment to accept weak financial aid services. Moreover, adult learners, who constitute a crucial audience, may simply give up if they feel they are being passed around or talking with someone who takes no personal interest in their success.

MARKETING AND COMMUNICATIONS

Decisions about how to handle marketing and communications are more complex. Staff members who are solidly professional in these areas are extremely valuable but not always easily found. Too often, campuses have tried to get by with existing staff, assigning marketing and communications to someone who has an interest and appears to have some skill. That may have been acceptable in the past, but it is risky today.

I have seen unbelievably bad web pages and brochures that were developed by branch campuses, and the campus leadership didn't recognize the problems. In my opinion, unless a campus is large enough to hire an experienced professional, or gets extremely lucky, the quality of the product may directly harm recruitment efforts. Moreover, it appears to me that non-professionals typically work more from intuition than from good research. In increasingly competitive environments, professionalism matters.

Unfortunately, flipping the arrangement around has its own problems. If marketing and communication support are provided only from the main campus, it is likely that some of the important nuances at the branch will be missed. This is especially true if the branch is at considerable distance from the main campus or if the branch student population's backgrounds and goals are quite different from those of main campus students.

Toward the end of my service as vice president, I thought we developed a good solution for the centralize-decentralize challenge. We hired a professional communications person through my office, to serve the campuses and Lifelong Learning, but located her in the main campus communications office. Her work was guided by our priorities, but she was in a good position to make sure our "products" were consistent with institutional standards and messages.

(I want to be careful here. Each campus had competent, dedicated individuals, but they were relatively isolated and not consistently in touch with the university's central staff. Working in isolation, as an office of one, each of them received little feedback and few professional development opportunities. Given that we had five campuses and approximately nine thousand students, we could support a central office person, accountable to me, as well as the local staff, accountable to the campus deans.)

The person we hired brought significant improvement to the editorial quality of branch press releases and the like, although she did not write many of them. She also did a good job of keeping main campus staff conscious of our existence. For example, the main campus developed a very successful marketing campaign called "The Promise Campaign," and I was pleased by the commitment to make sure that the campaign would have an appropriate branch campus expression.

There is no way I can fully explore this topic, because generalizations seem bound to be wrong. A highly motivated main campus communications person may do perfectly well, if he or she has good ties to branch campus personnel, whereas a questionably competent branch person could miss many opportunities and turn off prospective students.

I do believe that branches generally will be most effective at marketing when they emphasize bringing outstanding opportunities to the local community that are grounded in the historical excellence of the main campus. To put it in more current terms, branches should exploit the main campus brand, while bringing an element of accessibility and affordability to students for whom that is a critical element.

I worked with one dean who believed the exact opposite. He told me that his goal was to create a message in his community that the local branch was *different* than the main campus. He believed that his community found the main campus intimidating and cold, and to the extent that people believed the branch was like the main campus, that was a bad thing. He also was an aggressive marketer, and viewed the main campus as competition, a perspective I never shared.

Not surprisingly, main campus offices did not trust this dean, and they had quite a few stories to justify that mistrust. On the other hand, his campus grew steadily from year to year, so draw your own conclusions.

As usual for Ohio State, in Mansfield we handled things locally, but with very few complications, because of the shared culture. I remember a great advertising campaign, produced shortly after I left, that built around the line "The best are Buckeyes." During a campus visit, our marketing/communications person arranged for a picture of John Cooper (head football coach) and

Archie Griffin (only player ever to win two Heisman trophies) with several high school valedictorians and salutatorians who were enrolling at our campus. I thought it was a great line, but it wouldn't work most places.

To decide on an approach, keep in mind that marketing, especially, is not an area where "something is better than nothing." Bad work is *far* worse than no work at all. Moreover, unskilled marketers can waste a great deal of money. I suppose, then, my advice is to take time to get this one right, question your intuitions and past practice, and don't be afraid to invest some money in this critical area. Done well, both marketing and communications are an *investment*, not simply an expense.

As a final point, although I believe professionalism and experience is extremely important in the areas of marketing and communications, I also believe that the chief administrator of a branch campus *must* have final approval over any ads, press releases, brochures, or general recruitment practices. That approval is a critical check and balance to make sure that all messages resonate with the local community and student markets.

RETENTION SERVICES

It is a truism that retention of current students is less expensive than recruiting new students. To that I add that an access mission ought to imply a powerful commitment to student success. Nevertheless, the cost of retention programs seems always to be an issue on branch campuses, and there are legal considerations, as well.

On the legal side, I'm surprised by how many campuses give lip service, at best, to meeting ADA requirements and assuring that all students have an opportunity for success. I understand that requirements for disability services are confusing and perplexing for many administrators. Moreover, given the small size of many branches, as well as their marginal financial condition, meeting the letter of the law can be difficult. Most branches seem to have a disability services person on staff, but that staff member is not always well trained or supported from the main campus. Take care not to be tripped up by ignorance on this important issue.

I do encourage leaders to be pragmatic about retention services. In this area, impact assessment is important. I see no point in providing any specific service in the absence of evidence that it is being used and making a difference. Neither do I believe in having offices open just in case someone comes by, unless there is evidence to show that significant drop-ins happen.

In my opinion, academic advising is the single most important retention tool, and there is no doubt that financial aid has a profound effect on branch campus retention. In fact, with regard to financial aid, too often I've talked with or heard about students who withdrew because they lacked a very small amount of money to fully cover their bills. In Mansfield, we maintained a revolving small loan fund, administered by the Admissions/Financial Aid Office, which served as a great tool to get students over a financial aid hump or some other problem.

I've sometimes used tutoring as an example of a service that too often is provided without evidence that it makes a difference for more than a rare student. On-site child care, which almost always is an expensive service, can be another example. Either or both may, in fact, be important for retention, and it is not my intention to suggest otherwise. What I object to is services provided out of "moral" conviction, without evidence that they have a significant effect.

OTHER SERVICES

Branch campuses may provide a wide range of services, but in today's environment, all services and cost centers should be expected to demonstrate an impact on recruitment or retention.

Even maintaining pleasant, safe buildings and grounds should be thought of as supporting student success. I believe that buildings and grounds, as well as a safe environment, do make a difference, and I've always encouraged maintenance, custodial, grounds, and security staff to consider their work as important to the mission. That doesn't mean the campus leadership should go overboard on spending.

In addition to gathering evidence of impact, I believe it is important to survey students, faculty, and staff about services. Sometimes ideas emerge that are worth testing, and keeping track of suggestions from students, especially, made a difference on the campuses where I served.

For example, in Mansfield, we introduced "drop-in" advising to accommodate students with quick questions. Each advisor committed a certain amount of time to be on drop-in duty, and students with questions queued up in the reception area. If it turned out that a student's question was too complex for a quick response, he or she was referred for an advising appointment. The idea came from the initial survey we did of advising effectiveness that I mentioned above.

In another example, mentioned previously, some adult learners came to us with a concern that our computer lab was not open enough hours at times they could use. We made some changes and began keeping data on usage by hour, and as I recall, we were able to meet their needs without increasing staffing cost.

My point is simply to be practical and data driven, when it comes to services. Even the library is a good example of how things can vary. Today, libraries serve functions very different from those when I was at the beginning of my career. The nature of libraries and library services may vary quite a lot, depending on mission and enrollment, but it is important to get it right.

Security is a serious concern for many campuses, and it is yet another area that calls for pragmatic, cost-effective decisions that also respect legitimate concerns. I remember a faculty member coming into my office in Lancaster, very upset, and informing me that we needed to add full-time security officers at the campus. His reason was that someone had grabbed a staff member's purse while she was out of her office. It turned out that the staff member had left the purse in plain view, without closing the door, when she walked away.

I pointed out that the odds of a security officer being present at exactly the right time and place were quite low, so his solution to create a significant continuing expense needed to be considered carefully. We did hold a campus discussion about security, because we had also experienced vandalism in our food service area and a fight between students in the parking lot one evening.

Ohio University police did a security audit of the campus and made a number of recommendations, including improvements to lighting in the parking lots, trimming back certain bushes, installing security cameras, and so on. We met with the Lancaster police, and reaffirmed their commitment to respond to calls from the campus.

My point isn't that we came up with the "right" solution for all branch campuses, but it seemed appropriate for our situation. At Mansfield, we had full-time, 24/7 uniformed security officers. However, that campus is located in a relatively isolated area, outside town; enrolled more than four thousand students (combining the university branch and the co-located technical college); and had at least eight buildings, at the time I was there. In addition, our law enforcement support came from the Ohio Highway Patrol, which did not always have an officer in proximity to respond to emergencies.

As a different example, I remember visiting the Raymond Walters Campus of the University of Cincinnati, years ago, and at least at the time, university police provided branch campus security services. In that situation, the main campus and the branch were only a few miles apart, so response time could be quite fast, and patrol cars regularly drove around campus.

As still another option, I visited a branch that had trained student "security." These students actually were a preventive measure. They carried radios and wore a bright orange jacket, with "SECURITY" on the back. They walked around parking lots and through buildings, and they could assist students with a car problem or some other issue, but they were required to call in any disturbances, rather than responding directly.

The lesson here is that branches have options for providing needed services, and the most reasonable solution can depend on many things. What almost never makes sense is to create a service that is expensive, simply to satisfy some people's preferences or strongly held convictions, without thoughtful exploration.

WHO SHOULD MANAGE SERVICES?

As I mentioned above, branch campuses typically offer only a subset of programs and services that are available at the main campus. In general, local services should be those that have a direct impact on recruitment or retention, both of which require sensitivity to the student population and to community characteristics. Backroom services, typically, should be centralized, usually at the main campus.

Especially in my consulting work, I encounter at least as much debate and disagreement over the management of services as I do over academic programs and course schedules. From a branch campus perspective, staff members tend to feel that main campus staff treat branch campus students as a lower priority than main campus students. They believe that office hours and procedures are too often designed for main campus convenience rather than for branch campus needs, and that main campus staff are dismissive or condescending in their attitudes toward branch campus staff.

From the opposite perspective, main campus staff members often perceive branch staff as inconsistent or lax in enforcing policies and procedures and believe that training and communication challenges require keeping branch campus staff on a short leash. Also, in almost all cases, main campus offices are understaffed, a fact that branch staff members often either don't understand or don't find especially relevant; lean staffing levels, however, affect student services on all campuses.

Because this book is about branch campuses, I'm sure my perspective will favor the concerns of branch staff; but I emphasize that, if the goal is to see branch campuses increase enrollment, then the branch perspective *ought* to be given priority. Still, it would be unfair to suggest that branch campus staff members are somehow more dedicated, skilled, or compassionate than main campus staff. The environments are different, with important implications for how each perceives mission and service.

In my experience, I've seen three general approaches to managing branch student services. The approach I generally favor is to establish a student services office at the branch, with staff members accountable to the chief administrator of the campus. There may be a director of student services, or the equivalent, who is responsible for a wide range of activities, including admissions, advising, financial aid, learning support, and any relevant aspects of student life.

A second approach is to locate staff at the branch campus, but reporting to various department heads at the main campus. Thus, admissions staff are accountable to the main campus admissions office, financial aid to the main campus financial aid office, and so on. The local chief administrators are *not* the supervisors, although they may develop significant influence through relationships at both their own campus and the main campus.

At campuses I've visited, this second approach appears to work fairly well, although it surely lacks efficiency. Success depends on how well people get along, how far the branch is located from the main campus, and how clearly executive officers emphasize the importance of providing good service to branch campus students.

At the very least, in this arrangement, the branch administrator should have a dotted line relationship to any and all local staff. Everyone should understand that the branch administration has both the responsibility and the authority to assure efficient, student-centered operations that meet the needs of their audience. Conflicts may emerge between the main campus and its branches, of course, and there should be an established procedure to resolve differences.

The third approach is to locate only the most minimal staffing at the branch campus. There may be, say, a director, an assistant director, plant support, and office support. Everyone else works from the main campus, visiting the branch on occasion but mostly working with students over the telephone or through e-mail. Video conferencing and instant messaging can help improve responsiveness and a reasonable comfort level for branch campus students.

As I've suggested, the third approach probably makes sense for backroom services. It isn't especially important, for instance, that someone on the branch campus catalogue library holdings; and financial aid needs assessment, bursar functions, and most registrar functions can be centralized. In addition, it may make perfect sense to have academic unit representatives visit the branch on a regular basis, to supplement whatever services are provided on site.

I firmly believe that admissions counseling (not processing), professional academic advising, financial aid counseling, and any other service that requires what I'd call a "counseling perspective" should be provided by staff on site. Visits and technology are not good enough. I tend to feel the same way about learning support (tutoring, writing center, math lab, and so on). I've seen institutions with branches or centers that are too small to support full-time services, and sometimes multiple branches need to share staff. Consistent, predictable services matter more than a full-time presence, in my opinion.

For all that, what *really* sets me off is too much main campus control over marketing and recruiting. If all marketing and recruitment is controlled from the main campus, with little or no input from the branch administration, then that should change. If there is significant interaction, and the branch administration has substantial authority, including the authority to veto bad ideas, then that is at least an improvement.

To be sure, the main campus has legitimate and significant interest in coordinating all marketing and communications, so I encourage strong ties between the main campus and the branch, especially with regard to marketing. Main campus review of marketing materials, for example, strikes me as quite reasonable.

If branch campus enrollment growth is a priority, then leadership needs to be empowered to make that happen. However, I also believe that branch campuses should pay their way, so campus enrollment is a consideration, with regard not only to which services are provided, but also to how they are staffed. A strong revenue-sharing model, such as I will discuss in chapter 8, can allow staffing at the branch campus to evolve as enrollment grows.

A BRANCH ADMINISTRATOR'S PERSPECTIVE ON MAIN CAMPUS STUDENT SUPPORT STAFF

I'm grateful that I spent a dozen years working on the main campus at Ohio University, or my attitude toward main campus staff might be much more negative. I want to offer some thoughts that may be thoroughly unappreciated by some, but I believe the differences in mission, along with simple human nature, can help explain why branch campus staff are often so frustrated.

In general, main campus offices are oriented toward traditional-aged undergraduate students. Thus, I found that graduate school and medical school administrators, continuing education administrators, and others who worked with audiences that could not readily stand in line between (sometimes) 9:00 and 4:00 often shared my frustrations. On many occasions I asked branch staff members, at a variety of institutions, what created their greatest frustrations. Almost to a person, the reply was that they were frustrated any time they had to tell a student to contact the main campus, because they expected the student would not be well served.

Now, I must quickly add that I've seen poor service from branch campus staff, and I've known main campus staff members who consistently went the extra mile for branch campus students. But as a generalization, I believe students receive better service on branch campuses than on main campuses.

Again, if I am correct, it is not because main campus staff members are incompetent or lack dedication. Rather, all the variables line up to create a difference in perspective and consciousness. For example, if an institution has 15,000 main campus undergraduates (90 percent of whom are between 18 and 22), 2,000 graduate students, and 1,500 branch campus students, how are services to be prioritized?

Add in the facts that the main campus office probably is understaffed and that nonresidential students are less visible on a daily basis, and one can appreciate why processes, office hours, and time invested per student are geared toward the largest group of students. In addition, branch students, like continuing education and graduate students, often have atypical issues that do not fit neatly into categories. It is a question of priorities, not concern.

I've also heard "philosophical" arguments on this issue. Sometimes branch campus staff seem to do too much hand holding, according to people on the main campus, and part of becoming educated is learning to take personal responsibility for rules, processes, and finding information. Nevertheless, as a friend of mine says, it often seems as if his main campus contacts are looking for a reason to say "no." It ends conversations and saves time.

At the bottom line, branch campuses typically feel the pressure of competition more keenly than staff in equivalent positions on the main campus. Because there is a lack of departmentalization on many branch campuses, branch staff members may see more clearly how processes break down at departmental lines, or how students feel passed around by people they do not know. Branch staff may also feel caught in the middle, because students take out their frustrations on them, not necessarily understanding why it takes so long to resolve issues.

Pushing the point, branch campuses are about access and opportunity, and many branch students are individuals who face personal and financial challenges to their education. When processes and rules throw up barriers, branch campus students are more likely than main campus students to walk away or to choose an alternative institution. Branch campus staff members are embedded in this "access" environment, and they often work more intimately with their students. They may not see particular problems as often as staff members on the main campus, failing to appreciate how disruptive those problems can be in the relevant main campus office.

I realize I am painting a more critical picture of main campus staff members, so let me add that there is a special place in hell for branch campus staff who are not service oriented. That, in my opinion, is unforgiveable, because service and support are essential to enrollment success.

Regardless, this is a book about branch campuses, so I don't apologize for writing from their point of view. (I'll be more critical of branch campuses in a later chapter.) I sincerely believe that many main campus administrators and support staff could learn a lot from their branch campus staff, and those lessons might be all the more important as competition increases. At the very least, the better branch campus and main campus people know each other, the better they will understand each other and be able to serve students.

It is worth the time and trouble to get people together on a regular basis. At Ohio University, we brought student support staff to the main campus about six times a year for daylong meetings with people from various offices. I'm not sure those meetings were fascinating to our staff members, but they were helpful. I also believe that main campus staff members who support branch campus students should visit the campuses, at least once or twice a year, and talk directly with branch students.

SOME ADVICE TO BRANCH CAMPUS STAFF

In my opinion, one of the great strengths of branch campuses is the lack of traditional departmentalization. This applies both to faculty and to staff, and I consider it to be one of the defining characteristics of my "idealized" branch. Whereas main campus departments may be in different buildings and interact only as needed, on branch campuses student support staff typically work in close proximity, and they often are cross-trained, especially at smaller campuses.

One of the steps we took in Mansfield, of which I was most proud, was to create a single student support "staff." Admissions, Financial Aid, and Academic Advising were in a single space, sharing a reception area. Career counseling was nearby, and we included Student Activities and our writing lab, math lab, and study skills staff in meetings. All of those staff members reported directly to me, and my office was right next to the Business Office, as well.

In Lancaster, we had a director of student services, and virtually all of those services reported to him. I missed the direct interaction, but I count myself fortunate to have been so involved in Mansfield, because I learned a great deal. On both campuses, I led the marketing effort and kept close involvement with communications, although it was only in Lancaster that communications reported directly to me. Of course, in Lancaster I also was responsible for the physical plant, the campus budget, and fund raising.

My point is simply that working on a branch campus is a remarkable opportunity. There is no doubt that a main campus appointment carries higher status than an equivalent appointment on a branch campus, but the *learning* potential across elements of the institution tend to be greater on branch campuses, and I wish more people had the opportunity to benefit from that experience.

For early career individuals, the branch campus experience can be especially enlightening. In Mansfield, we hired quite a few people early in their careers, some of them just out of graduate school. Some of those individuals are still there, and others moved on to more traditional paths. Regardless, their work in Mansfield necessarily implied close relationships with people working across the student support spectrum, and it also gave them far more opportunities to work with faculty members than would have occurred elsewhere at such an early career stage.

I recall that some individuals moved on precisely because they wanted a more specialized role, and I remember one person telling me that she wanted more distance from the faculty (go figure). However, at least at the time, they recognized the value of two or three years on a branch campus.

For those who are hired locally, and perhaps with less formal preparation for academic work, my advice is a little different. I've seen a number of situations in which a branch campus, because it followed main campus policies on compensation, was one of the highest-paying employers in a small town. As a result, turnover was extremely low, both for professional staff and, especially, for classified staff.

I have no criticism of "homegrown" staff members, because their dedication tends to be second to none, but I encourage branch and institutional leaders to be sure these individuals have ongoing opportunities to learn more about the main campus and to attend conferences and workshops, where they can hear about best practices and new ideas.

Working on a branch campus is challenging in many ways. Staff members, especially classified staff members, tend not to fit neatly into main campus job descriptions. That sometimes leads to unfair treatment, especially on compensation. Very often, opportunities for advancement are extremely limited, and people risk becoming stale if senior administrators aren't careful to maintain a stimulating environment. However, we often say that branch campus staff members wear many hats, thus keeping their jobs full of variety and challenge. Therein lie both the joy and the frustration.

7
Agendas and Stakeholders

EVERYONE HAS HIS OR HER POINT OF VIEW. Main campus faculty members may perceive branch campuses as a threat to enrollment in their own courses, an unwelcome obligation that stretches staffing capacity, or a lesser-quality option to attending the "real" university. Main campus administrators may not think much about branches at all, but when they do, it is likely that they will view them as creating extra work or needing to be kept on a short leash, so they don't "run amok."

On branch campuses, both faculty and staff members may talk about the difficulty of pursuing an access mission, given the neglect, if not direct interference, from the main campus. Branch campus students may feel like neglected stepchildren, with their need for specific courses at reasonable times going unfilled.

When it comes to branch campuses, there are so many stakeholders that I'm amazed at how well many campuses perform. Their success testifies to the hard work and dedication of branch campus faculty and staff, aided and abetted by those main campus individuals who, for whatever reason, decide to be helpful rather than oppositional. At the same time, given all the complications, barriers, and politics, these campuses could do even better if they did not encounter so many obstacles.

For that reason, I chose to include a separate chapter on stakeholders and their agendas. In my opinion, branch campus faculty and staff too often underappreciate the complexity of stakeholder interests and how those interests affect decision making. Stakeholders matter, because they have agendas and the power to influence events. If their agendas have the potential to help or hurt an institution, then they will attract the attention of the leadership. Thus, faculty members' agendas matter because faculty deliver the "product": the academic program. However, they also matter because an angry faculty can create disruption and suck up a lot of time.

AT THE INSTITUTIONAL LEVEL

Think of all the stakeholders the president has to keep in mind. There are the executive officers, who tend to think and act according to their own segments' interests; there are the deans who focus on their budgets, program reputation, and departmental issues; there are the academic department chairs, sitting between the academic leadership (provost and dean) and their faculty.

For the president, the main campus faculty is a stakeholder in its own right, and we need to acknowledge students (main campus students, I mean here), as well as parents and potential employers. There are trustees, alumni, donors, athletics coaches/ programs, and community leaders; there are accrediting agencies, both for the institution and for many individual programs; there are state-level policy makers, boards, legislators, and agencies that have something to say about the institution.

Lest we forget, there may be one or more satellite campuses, as well as students attending the institution through online courses and programs. Given so many stakeholders, not to mention the traditions, enrollments, and budgets that are priorities on the main campus, is it any wonder that branch campuses are not top-of-mind for the president? It isn't that he or she doesn't care; rather, branches are competing with an enormous array of entities for attention.

It is intriguing to think about the fact that most of these stakeholders, while acknowledging the others, believe their interests should be weighted more heavily than they seem to be. Yet the president has to give each its due and seek a way to balance the use of resources. I emphasize this because the influence of these stakeholders absolutely affects branch campuses. Indeed, branch campuses have their own stakeholders, but branch leaders need to be aware of those involved at the institutional level as well.

AT THE BRANCH CAMPUS LEVEL

Nearly all the institutional-level stakeholders are replicated at the branch. Generally, branch campus chief administrators have counterparts in each of the main campus groups. Thus, there typically are faculty members, staff members, students, alumni, perhaps donors, perhaps an advisory board, community members, political leaders, and so on.

I've known branch administrators who claimed that they were, in effect, campus presidents, and sometimes their stature in the local community is such that their day-to-day experience is "presidential." Although a few branch leaders actually have the title of president, I've yet to see an example where anyone on the main campus showed a branch administrator the deference implied by that title. (Keep in mind that I am talking about multi-campus institutions, not true systems with a relatively high level of independence at each campus.)

There are two problems with thinking of a branch administrator as being a president. First, several of the main campus stakeholders (e.g., provost, deans, faculty, administrative department heads) have sufficient authority to sharply limit branch campus autonomy. A branch campus chief administrator doing battle with, say, the university registrar is likely to get a lesson in the limits of his or her power.

Second, most stakeholders with a direct interest in the branch campus do not have the impact of main campus stakeholders. A local advisory board, for example, will not have the authority of the institution's board of trustees. Community leaders and local employers probably will not be able to influence curriculum even as much as do those with more direct ties to the main campus. Nevertheless, leading a branch campus requires understanding the interests of stakeholders, both locally and at the main campus.

In this chapter, I explore the impact of stakeholders from a fresh angle. In later chapters, I will consider financial issues and the role of the chief administrator, before concluding with some thoughts on the future of branch campuses.

PRESIDENTS AND PROVOSTS

What I haven't mentioned so far is that presidents and provosts also are important stakeholders. (Together with "provost" I mean to include those with the title of vice president for academic affairs.) To begin with, some branch chief administrators report directly to the president, although it is more common to report to the provost. Sometimes the reporting line is more indirect, to a vice president for administration or student affairs, for example, or to a dean for undergraduate studies. Occasionally, the reporting line is to the chief continuing education administrator.

Whether the reporting relationship is direct or not, the president's and provost's perception of branch campuses is critical. Generally, I've found presidents to be supportive of their branches, partly from genuine commitment to the access mission, but also because branches can expand political support, generate revenue for various non-branch-specific purposes, and expand the overall size and significance of their institutions.

Only rarely do presidents invest significant time and energy in branch development, however. In most cases the branches are too small—but keep in mind that presidents also do not invest a lot of time in other individual elements of the institution. That's the role of other executive officers. I realize that many branch leaders feel neglected by the president, but they need to understand that the "neglect" is a matter of available time, and many main campus leaders also feel they deserve more attention.

On the other hand, I've found provosts to be more of a mixed bag. Personally, I had good relationships with the provosts I knew in my branch campus–related career, but in my consulting work, branch leaders express frustration more often with their provost than with their president.

Of course, it is likely that branch leaders have more contact with the provost than with the president, and often the issues of concern involve competing with other units for financial support. Because many provosts have a very traditional academic background, their concerns lean toward issues related to budget control, academic rankings, and almost anything other than entrepreneurship, which is critical to the understanding of branches, online programs, and other continuing education–type initiatives.

Finally, keep in mind that presidents and provosts sometimes have personal agendas, and those agendas may not be consistent with investing resources in branch campuses. Benign neglect is one thing, but branch campuses are unlikely to thrive if the executive leadership views them as an exploitable cash cow or a political irritant.

FACULTY AS STAKEHOLDERS

Many people consider faculty members and students to be the most important stakeholders for any institution, and although I might argue that staff members, as stakeholders, should not be underestimated, let's accept the point. Both faculty members and students may try to claim first rank, but that type of debate is a waste of breath. Faculty members carry the history and culture of an institution more than any other group, whereas there is an obvious truth in the statement that, without students, there would be no institution.

A significant challenge for branch campuses is that faculty members actually can be subdivided to the point that one could argue (or worry) that each individual faculty member is a stakeholder in his or her own right. Especially on branches, a faculty member may be the only representative on campus in a disciplinary specialty. For sure, one must recognize that the branch faculty and the main campus faculty have divergent interests.

In a world of shared governance, faculty claim to "own" the curriculum, but you can bet that the faculty being referred to is located on the main campus, not the branch. Even if branch campus faculty have a voice on curriculum committees, most will be doing well if they can make sure that branch needs are considered when changes are being discussed. Moreover, curriculum ownership tends to be vested at the departmental level, with some grudging acknowledgment that college-level colleagues have a right at least to review and comment on proposals.

Just to emphasize that individual faculty members carry influence, I've seen many situations in which a main campus faculty member claimed that a specific course belonged to him or her, and *no one else could teach it*, especially on a branch campus. Sometimes such individuals are sufficiently dedicated that they will come out to the branch or teach over a video system, but not always. Interestingly, I've also seen faculty members who would "allow" their own doctoral student to teach a needed course at the branch but would block a branch campus faculty member with a PhD in the discipline from teaching it.

For present purposes, I simply want to recognize that faculty members, as stakeholders, carry a lot of clout, and the way they use that clout depends on the institution and the willingness of deans and others to step up if someone is being unreasonable or capricious. In my experience, deans and chairs are reluctant to intervene on behalf of a branch campus need, unless their unit faces a loss of revenue from courses or programs that are not being offered.

This issue is becoming more problematic as faculty members develop online course options. At Ohio University, several years ago, we had good data indicating that main campus students were enrolling in an online statistics course developed and taught through a branch campus. To his credit, the dean of Arts and Sciences did not object to the online offering (although he might feel obliged to object when the institution moves to responsibility-centered budgets), but he was concerned that the department chair needed good enough information to make decisions about how many sections of this course to offer on the main campus each term. This will be an interesting issue to watch.

STUDENTS AS STAKEHOLDERS

When we say that colleges and universities face a "buyers' market," we are recognizing that students, as well as their parents, employers, and others who influence students' decisions, have more options than in the past. Although the so-called traditional students (eighteen to twenty-two years old, attending full time) may still prefer a residential undergraduate experience, adult learners, as well as younger students for whom a residential experience is problematic, may prefer commuting, attending in the evening, enrolling in online or hybrid courses, or other options.

Part of the value of branch campuses is that they serve different audiences than most main campuses serve; they provide services and meeting space that are not available online. In the final chapter, I will speculate about the future of branch campuses, but for the moment I want to make a very practical point: most colleges and universities that are attractive only to full-time, daytime students are in for a rough ride. It will be difficult to impossible to cover the full cost of educating and supporting those students. Surviving, never mind thriving, will depend on attracting various groups of students, and many potential students' choices may be determined by how far they have to drive, how much they have to spend, or how much flexibility in scheduling and the use of technology is provided.

Students have always been central stakeholders, and those of us committed to access surely care about their interests. However, as students have more choices than ever to support meeting their goals, competing effectively to attract enrollment requires an understanding of student needs that will be a challenge for all too many institutions. All of the posturing and stumbling of legislators, trustees, and accreditors aside, students' choices will determine which institutions thrive and which do not.

TRUSTEES

If there is one extremely important stakeholder that most people underestimate, it is the institution's board of trustees. I did not appreciate the active role of trustees until I became a vice president.

I first had an opportunity to address trustees when I was leading the Mansfield Campus Faculty Assembly and the trustees met on our campus. I remember it as a terribly serious thing, very formal, with my remarks written and rehearsed. Later, at Ohio University, the relationship became more personal and comfortable, but there were times when the trustees' authority became clear and demanded respect.

In Ohio, trustees are appointed by the governor to serve nine-year terms. They (not a search committee) actually hire the president, who then appoints other executive officers and deans.

I emphasize this because, although some people like to believe that administrators are appointed to do whatever it is that faculty members don't want to do, there is another, quite different, point of view.

In essence, the power of trustees lies in the fact that they have a fiduciary responsibility that must be met, both legally and functionally. They hire the president, who typically has a contract, but nevertheless serves at the trustees' pleasure. Rarely will one hear a president speak publicly about managing his or her relationship with the board, but it takes quite a bit of time, and it affects significant leadership decisions. My sense is that most boards and presidents have strongly positive relationships, but managing board relationships is important for the entire institution.

Public and private institutions work differently with their trustees, and there is a literature on developing effective boards and board-administration relationships. I am not an expert on the subject, but I feel sympathy for leaders of institutions that have elected trustees. Standing for election seems more common at community colleges than at universities, but in either case it strikes me as a very bad approach to governance, with too much risk of eccentric decisions by voters.

BRANCH CAMPUS ADVISORY BOARDS

Many institutions create local advisory boards to support their branch campuses, and sometimes there are program-specific boards, as well. Advisory boards are an excellent way to build community ties, but surprisingly, some campuses shy away from creating them. When asked, I always favor establishing boards, but shaping a meaningful role for their members is challenging.

An advisory board is not a governing board, and that presents the biggest challenge. To be of maximum value to a branch, advisory board members should be influential members of their community. Such individuals are well known, can serve as effective advocates for the campus, and are likely to appreciate at least some of the issues faced by the campus leadership. (They most definitely will not understand or appreciate our glacial search processes or the entire notion of shared governance!)

Potential members probably have experience serving on nonprofit boards of trustees, but the role of advisory board members tends to be more ambiguous. There are few voting issues, and members have almost no input on academic issues, the most substantive of which are addressed on the main campus.

Most branch campus chief administrators with whom I've discussed advisory boards struggle to find a meaningful agenda for their boards, and that may help explain the reluctance of some people to create boards that do not already exist. Giving influential people a false sense of their authority seems wrong.

Nevertheless, I have experienced firsthand the impact individual board members can have when a branch campus needs strong advocates. These are people who can pick up a telephone and speak directly to legislators, local political leaders, and potential donors.

At Ohio University we recognized two specific areas in which we committed to seeking support from our advisory boards. The first was in the hiring and evaluation of the campus dean (chief administrator). In theory, we could hire or fire the dean against the wishes of the local board, but we certainly never hired a dean without the board's support, to my knowledge. (We never fired any deans, with or without board support, in my years of service.) The second area of formal consultation was on capital projects. These projects were not routine, but we felt we should not pursue projects that lacked community support.

Unfortunately, my impression is that most advisory board meetings become the proverbial "dog and pony show." It is important that board members develop familiarity with the programs and services at the campus, because one of their contributions is to listen to community voices and, in turn, help other people understand what is available at the branch. However, too much sitting and listening will be frustrating to people used to being in charge.

Over the years, I concluded that most advisory boards should meet only a few times each year, perhaps quarterly. Brief updates from campus leaders, along with a presentation from a faculty member or one of the areas of student support, were well received. I also found that boards appreciated hearing from a main campus representative and having an opportunity to ask questions about main campus affairs, as well as to express their concerns on almost anything from the football team to the need for more courses and programs at the branch campus.

Other than the extremely rare use of political and personal clout, the best advice I received from community advisory boards was on the subject of marketing. In my experience, there is no one-size-fits-all approach to marketing branch campuses. So much depends on the programs offered and the most effective channels for connecting to various audiences. Community business leaders, and especially owners of successful small businesses, were invaluable advisors on marketing issues, and the energy always seemed to increase in our conversations when marketing was the topic.

I appreciate the concerns that administrators have about the role of advisory boards and how best to work with them, but not having such a board misses a great opportunity for connection and support. Some established, formal connection respects the community as a stakeholder and provides an opportunity to manage communication in a positive manner.

AGENDAS

To repeat, stakeholders matter because they have agendas and the power to influence events. Sometimes it seems as if those agendas are not in the best interest of higher education, whether they come from a love of power, an extreme social or political position, or some misguided commitment to one constituency over others.

Thus, I've seen presidents who believed (wrongly, in my opinion) that they were going to lead their second-tier public university to becoming one of the nation's premier research universities, and as a result badly harmed their institution by emphasizing research too heavily, overreaching on athletic programs, and generating staggering levels of institutional debt. I've seen examples of donors trying to push a personal agenda that may have come from genuine passion but risked creating an imbalance that was inconsistent with an institution's strengths.

I could go on, with examples related to athletics, political grandstanding, academic program arrogance, and the like. Fortunately, although egos definitely come into play, most of this particular type of drama is less common on branch campuses. The *creation* of branch campuses may have a great deal of drama associated with it, and I think we may see more drama associated with closing or threatening to close branches in response to budget pressures.

To be sure, effectively advancing the branch campus mission requires understanding that all these diverse stakeholders have their respective interests, and that the principles of effective negotiation apply to accomplishing almost anything significant. Some people or groups may have deeply self-serving or uninformed agendas, and nothing is more frustrating than wrestling over an agenda that does not embrace the best interests of the institution.

Remember, however, that each stakeholder believes his or her concerns are legitimate and important. Leaders occasionally come across people who have deliberately manipulative aims, but it happens more rarely than many people imagine. Stakeholders' interests may be selfish or uninformed, but when presenting their point of view, they believe they are addressing important matters.

A book on branch campuses is not the place to go into depth on organizational politics, but skillful assessment and negotiation are essential for making good things happen. In fact, success in academic administration probably depends most heavily on political agility and budget management. Note, by the way, that search committees rarely give great emphasis to those critical skills, contributing to what I might consider the miracle that anything works at all.

At the very least, branch administrators face a broad mix of stakeholders or constituencies, which means that they simply must be politically astute. This is especially true because the branch leadership faces these local and main campus stakeholders with relatively little ability to force any specific outcome.

The good news is that principles of negotiation are well established and most definitely teachable. My suggestion is to read and study well the basics of mutual gains, or interest-based, bargaining. Roger Fisher, William Ury, and Bruce Patton provide an excellent description of principles in their book, *Getting to Yes* (1991). I also highly recommend attending one of the seminars presented by The Program on Negotiation at Harvard Law School, if possible. I attended a two-day workshop some years ago and found it to be outstanding.

The significance of negotiation skills should not be underestimated. Stakeholders are interested in advancing their agendas, so it follows that those responsible for advancing the agenda of a branch campus need to persuade other key stakeholders that their interests will be served by supporting branch growth and development.

The term "interests" is important. Power stems from the ability to help other people realize their interests, so one's ability to recognize and speak to interests determines negotiation success, to a considerable degree.

COLLABORATION AND COMPROMISE

Negotiation is a common enough experience in life, but political environments in which authority and power are dispersed depend on negotiation to resolve almost any issue that comes up. Research universities may place more explicit emphasis on shared governance than many other types of institutions do, but the reality is that various stakeholders all must be respected in order for an institution to do well.

That doesn't mean that every stakeholder must be fully satisfied. Leaders should have a clear enough sense of mission and future opportunities to recognize when to stand firm and when to be open to influence. They need to appreciate the difference between posturing and the true exercise of power, as well as to know when it is better to lose the support of a particular individual or group than to compromise on important issues.

In my faculty years, I delivered dozens of programs on managing change and conflict, and I always encouraged people to recognize the preference for collaborative solutions to disagreements (the so called "win-win" solution). Interest-based bargaining increases the likelihood of finding those good long-term solutions.

Unfortunately, sometimes we are forced into a compromise, instead of arriving at a collaborative solution, simply because time is limited or no one has enough clout to force an issue. Too much compromise can be harmful to everyone's long-term interests, but sometimes compromise is the best solution available. Other outcomes, including walking away without an agreement, may be legitimate when collaboration isn't available as an option; it depends on what is at stake and what will be lost without an agreement.

Money, or the control of money and other resources, speaks loudly, as does political clout and personal credibility. In my opinion, however, the biggest challenge to collaborative negotiation tends to be time. Collaboration may require a series of meetings, research to explore the implications of proposed solutions, and time spent getting to know each other, in order to build trust. When plates are too full or staffing too lean, stakeholders may be forced to take what they can get and move on. Negotiation is not easy, and experience matters here, maybe more than in any other aspect of leadership.

8

Financing and Managing Budgets on Branch Campuses

I'M A DATA GUY. I LIKE NUMBERS, AT LEAST when they tell a story, and I enjoy trying to understand the story they want to tell. Given my education as an experimental psychologist, for years the numbers that intrigued me tied to my research; but in administration the numbers I studied represented budgets, enrollments, applications, and so on.

Over time, I believe I developed a good grasp of the way marketing, recruitment, retention, and student-driven course scheduling come together to generate revenue. In effect, I suppose I became more like continuing education administrators than most of those in traditional roles: whereas most administrators have expenditure budgets—allocations within which they make spending decisions—at both Ohio State and Ohio University, in my years, we had to earn the money we spent. Perhaps more importantly, we also got to keep most of the money we earned, to invest in growth and in partnership development.

Understanding the dynamic relationship between investment and growth is an important aspect of an entrepreneurial approach to higher education, and I believe branch campuses best add value when their leadership understands entrepreneurship. Moreover, making decisions as if only faculty members teaching students drives revenue is far too simplistic. One needs to respect the role of faculty members and to be sensitive to political realities in a shared-governance environment, but everyone has a role to play in the recruitment and retention of students, and all those efforts have an impact on revenue.

I talk a lot about "dwelling in the numbers," by which I mean that it takes time to recognize patterns and to evolve rules of thumb that can help anticipate positive or negative trends. In my opinion, most administrators fail to dwell in the numbers, thus missing the important clues that are critical to the future, as well as becoming excessively dependent on their finance people. It isn't enough simply to project expectations or to watch the bottom line, if one is going to use financial information effectively.

Writing about budget and financial matters is another challenge for me. I have strong feelings about the effective use of financial resources, and I believe I have a track record that entitles me to my opinions. On the other hand, I do not like arrogance or an attitude that one's own point of view is the only one that can be effective. So, people are free to agree or disagree with what I have to say.

This chapter will necessarily be more detailed than most, but unless you develop a financial model that creates the right incentives, growth on branch campuses will be difficult to achieve. My intention is to tell a story of my own experiences, as well as of some approaches to the funding of branch campuses that I believe to be flawed. From these experiences I draw a few general conclusions that extract key points that I hope will be of value to others. Please note that this chapter, more than most, may emphasize public universities over private nonprofits or community colleges, but the principles should apply to all sectors.

BUDGET LESSONS

In my first administrative position, as associate dean, I worked with a dean who was both a mathematician and an extraordinary budget manager, John Riedl. I learned a lot from John, and he gradually gave me at least nominal responsibility for larger pieces of our campus budget, in areas that fell under my responsibility. Ultimately, I was watching over approximately $2 million of our budget.

We also had excellent data on enrollment patterns. Not only did we get regular reports on applications and admissions, but we also tracked registrations every term, in every class, from week to week. Eventually, these data, along with detailed monthly budget reports, yielded a powerful picture of the campus.

When we started our work, in 1986, the campus was in a difficult enrollment and financial position. Dean Riedl always credited me with getting a handle on the class schedule; all those data allowed me to build a three-year projection of course offerings, to which we stuck closely. Growth in enrollment allowed us to try a few experiments each year, add options in general education, and increase opportunities for faculty to teach low-enrollment courses in their specialties.

In fact, I pass on a lot of the credit to our faculty, for their input and recommendations; to the dean, for insisting on key parameters that helped me stick to a plan; and to our academic advisors, who brought remarkable insight concerning good and bad enrollment choices. Over time, our class schedule became very cost efficient, yet we received fewer complaints from students about getting the courses they needed. We were a good team, all around, and it was satisfying work.

When I arrived in Lancaster, as dean, we also had challenges concerning enrollment and spending. The approach to mission was quite different than in Mansfield, and because our campus offered technical associate degrees, I could not apply some of the rules of thumb I had developed in Mansfield to the Lancaster context. Nevertheless, over the four years I was there, the staff stepped up in the same areas: marketing, prospect management, improved class scheduling, and retention. We went through some difficult program evaluations, but over time added more programs than we subtracted, and enrollment grew.

When I became vice president for Regional Higher Education at Ohio University, I was interested in seeing whether my experience with budgets would translate to being responsible for a much bigger number. It worked out fine, but the scale does change, going from approximately $7 million at Lancaster to $42 million for the entire system, including the Division of Lifelong Learning. (That budget grew to more than $70 million by the time I left.)

My predecessor as vice president, Jim Bryant, served in the position for twenty-four years, and I will be forever grateful to him for handing off a system that was very solid financially. He also "got" budgets, although we had different ideas about when and where to invest (spend). In my years as dean, I often heard people insist that Jim had hidden pots of money that he could draw on, when he so chose. We definitely had solid financial reserves, but I never found any evidence of "hidden pots."

THE WAY THINGS WORKED IN "MY DAY"

In general, during my thirty-five-year career at Ohio State and Ohio University, funding worked reasonably well for branch campuses, partly because the models rewarded growth, and many campuses were growing. Each campus received its own state support, based on credit-hour production (more on that later), and its own allocation of "capital money," which supported campus improvements and renovations.

Although there were variations in how the seven universities with branch campuses approached budgets, typically a campus was credited with its income, including from tuition and fees, and paid an overhead charge to the main campus in recognition of services received. The state's coordinating board for higher education, the Ohio Board of Regents (OBOR), watched over how universities worked with their branches, and the board staff was known to step in if a university began treating a branch campus as if it were a cash cow.

Funding models for higher education are changing in Ohio, as they are changing in most states, so this description of how things worked is necessarily historical. It is hard to say how the new models will affect branch campuses, but my first take is that the outcome will not be good. Newer models tend to focus on completion, which works to the disadvantage of access institutions, but my biggest concern is that OBOR seems to be less concerned about making sure that universities adequately fund their access campuses.

There is irony in all of this, given that policy makers want to see more people pursuing higher education, and the fastest-growing segment of higher education, in Ohio, has been the university branch/regional campuses. However, the campuses have no real voice outside their institutions, and I'd guess that no one asked some important questions as the new models were developed.

Back to my story: At Ohio University, nearly all of our money came through student tuition or state support. The state's funding formula actually had something like fifteen categories of subsidy, presumably based on cost of instruction, although branch campuses typically offered courses in only a few categories. There were various buffers and guarantees to prevent major problems, but generally, a campus's revenue was closely tied to credit-hour production.

Part of the branch concept, especially when its mission focuses on access, is that the cost of operation should be less than that for a freestanding institution, and, presumably, that reduced cost should be shared with students. Accordingly, undergraduate student tuition is significantly lower on the branch campuses than at the main campus, although it typically is significantly higher than at community colleges. In my years, branch tuition was about 60 percent of that on the main campus, so the difference was meaningful.

At Ohio University, our overhead charge to the main campus was 8 percent. We sometimes referred to the overhead as a "franchise fee," in part because there was no direct connection between the fee and any specific service. In my time, the overhead was charged only on gross revenue from tuition and state support. We did not pay overhead on development funds, grants, or most contract training.

Our 8 percent overhead was more or less typical in Ohio. There is no question that we received our money's worth. The brand value of the university's name alone would justify a fee, but we never could have had lower tuition and covered the full cost of operation on our own.

Unfortunately, from my perspective, because the overhead money went into the "Athens General Fund," academic and administrative department heads could not see a direct connection between branch campus overhead and their own budgets. And we did hear complaints, mostly from academic department chairs, who claimed they received no benefit from supporting branch campuses. Administrative departments generally supported us with no financial complaints, unless we were creating some unusual expense, in which case we sometimes directly funded the additional cost.

We also transferred money from the branch campuses to the main campus in two other ways. First, as mentioned above, over the years we agreed to support certain specific services that were important to us, beyond the general support provided by overhead but budgeted in someone else's area. For example, we helped support the interactive television center, covered some expenses in the College of Education that were directly linked to regional campus students, and so on. Second, we had a fund we called "splits," which amounted to modest profit sharing with those academic units that housed courses delivered at the branch campuses. Thus, splits provided an incentive to academic units to support the branch program, and it gave them a bit of a "slush fund," as one person described it, outside of their regular operating budget.

Total transfers to the main campus came to about 12 percent of our gross tuition and state support. In addition, our small central office staff cost about 1 percent of gross revenue, and we paid some other expenses centrally, either because it was cheaper to do so or because they tied to what I'd call "system priorities" (e.g., to support international travel, faculty research, and new initiatives). These system priorities came to roughly 7 percent of revenue.

In summary, all revenue generated by the branch campuses was credited to the campus that generated it. That gross revenue was "taxed" at approximately 20 percent, to cover overhead, other transfers, splits, the central office, and system priorities. The remaining 80 percent was available to the campuses, and the deans controlled most of that spending. We were doing responsibility-centered management before most people even knew what it was.

The major exception to the deans having a free hand was the funding of new positions, which required approval in the central office, partly to coordinate faculty specialties, but also to make sure that staff positions had stable funding sources for the future. Generally, if the money was available, new positions were approved.

At least in the eight years I served as vice president, this model worked very well. Each campus did have a control total for spending, but deans could move money across various budget lines, as necessary. If a campus overspent—and it was typical for one of the five campuses to be struggling to some extent in a given year—we would have a conversation and develop a plan to bring things back into line. My predecessor did things somewhat differently, but not dramatically so, with the result that Ohio University's campuses had well over thirty years of financial stability.

It is important to emphasize that absolutely no dollars flowed from the main campus to the university's branch campuses. On the contrary, we transferred more than $8 million to the main campus in my final year. Moreover, we funded our own capital/plant expenses and maintained our own reserves. As budgets became tighter, more hungry eyes started looking at our reserves. Although it was fair to raise concerns about our level of reserves, I believe the university also had a sweet deal in our approach. There was no risk to the main campus, considerable political value, meaningful outreach to a part of the state that had traditionally been underserved, and a nice seven-figure income stream as a dividend.

Capital funding for branch campuses can also be a challenge. In Ohio, in my day, capital funding was by formula, and each branch campus had an allocation. The level was typically $1–2 million, each biennium, and we could "save up" across biennia for larger projects. Given that campuses were built in the 1960s to early 1970s, the capital funds were more or less adequate for building maintenance, updates, and moderate renovations. It was more of a challenge to raise money for new buildings, unless enrollment grew so much that an exception to the capital funding formula could be justified. (In my years, one of our campuses grew enough to get new buildings; the others did not, but did accomplish significant renovations.)

LATER

When I left my position as vice president for Regional Higher Education at Ohio University to help develop our online programs, the senior central position title changed to executive dean, and the reporting line shifted from the president to the provost. (Actually, I created the executive dean position, but as a co-ordinating role, with the executive dean continuing to serve as dean of his campus. When I left, it became a full-time position.)

A number of other things changed with regard to standard practice, but enrollment stayed strong for the most part. Exactly how the funding will work with all the changes unfolding is impossible for me to know, and whether the campuses will continue to thrive remains to be seen. It seems certain that the campuses will have less budget autonomy.

Undeniably, I have strong feelings about branch campus finance, and I am deeply proud of the success we had at Ohio University for a very long time, including decades before I came along. Obviously, institutions can thrive with different approaches to their budgets, and I will try to extract a few essential recommendations in a chapter summary.

CONTRASTS WITH OHIO STATE

To my knowledge, all of the university branches in Ohio were funded the same way, in the years I was involved. The level of overhead payments varied across universities, as did other practices, but so far as I could tell, the bottom lines were roughly comparable.

When I was at Ohio State, we paid an overhead rate that was about the same as that at Ohio University. However, we did not routinely make other transfers of funds. I do know that we agreed to provide one college with some money, in exchange for delivery of its graduate program on our campus, but that was not a common practice at the time.

I feel sure that the context in which the campuses operated made an important difference to perspectives on money. For example, on the teaching side, Ohio State's branches rarely used faculty members from the main campus, whereas Ohio University relied on quite a few main campus instructors, hired on overload contracts. Perhaps, also, the fact that branch faculty members on Ohio State's campuses hold appointments in their main campus departments put less emphasis on money than might otherwise have been the case. Most department chairs considered branch campus faculty members to be part of "their" faculty.

Moreover, Ohio State is simply much larger and more complex than Ohio University. Thus, Ohio State's branch enrollment and revenue are a smaller piece of the pie than Ohio University's. At least 30 percent of the undergraduate enrollment at Ohio University is on the regional campuses, whereas the figure is closer to 15 percent, at Ohio State. Ohio State's sources of revenue, including everything from their hospitals, to grants and contracts, to athletics, yield much more money than is available at Ohio University. As long as the branch campuses balance their budgets, there is not much incentive at Ohio State to worry about grabbing a bigger piece of the branch income.

In my opinion, main campus support offices at both institutions accepted their responsibility to branch campus offices and students, with only minor complaints. I have especially positive memories about the proactive engagement of a number of offices at Ohio State, but I also was pleased with the cooperation of people at Ohio University, when called on. The fact that Ohio University offices more often asked for financial contributions reflected the difference in size, as well as a history of the central office saying "Yes."

My point is simply to note that the size of the institutions may have had a significant effect on revenue sharing. Note also that Ohio State did not have a central office for regional campuses, so each individual campus was that tub on its own bottom. At least when I was there, the Ohio State campuses had few of what I'd call "system priorities," and shortfalls in revenue needed to be addressed locally. On balance, I would be hard pressed to say that one institution's approach is better than the other's, given capable leadership in relevant roles.

ALTERNATIVE APPROACHES

As I began to talk more with branch campus administrators around the country, then went deeper through opportunities to serve as a consultant, I realized that the approach to funding we enjoyed in Ohio was not typical. It seems obvious to me that institutional funding should be based primarily on credit hours taught, but I assume people who live in other funding cultures might disagree.

One important advantage of the Ohio approach, at least, is that it allows for reinvestment in branch campuses as they grow. In addition, the overhead and other transfers we provided at Ohio University meant that the main campus also realized more revenue as branch campus income grew. People can and did argue that the main campus should have received an even bigger percentage of the income, and they may be right, but the critical thing was the flow of dollars from the branches to the main campus, and not the other way around.

Unfortunately, in my opinion, many institutions have financial models that actually discourage, rather than encourage, growth in courses and programs at branch campuses. The problem often begins with how the state funds its institutions.

In some states, institutions are funded through what I'll call "direct allocation." That is, there is no specific relationship between enrollment and funding. I'm sure the president argues for more support, when enrollment grows, but that puts the cart before the horse: grow and maybe you'll get more funding. Recently, as we've seen, legislatures have tended to cut funding, with the result that some institutions, in turn, have moved to reduce admissions. Not a great model for economic development in that state!

In at least some states, there may actually be a tie between enrollment and state allocations, but the allocation still is to the institution as a whole, and the total allocation available is capped. So, in an example with which I'm familiar, because the main campus is at or near its cap, further enrollment growth may not generate any additional state funds for the university. If the cap were raised, the main campus probably would grow to that level, so unless an allocation is made directly to the branch, there is no institutional incentive to support branch campus growth.

With regard to tuition, states seem to handle revenue in a couple of different ways. Some states do not allow institutions to keep the revenue from tuition. Instead, it returns to state coffers. However, my impression is that most do allow institutions to retain tuition revenue. If the institution retains tuition revenue, at least there is the possibility of developing business models to support enrollment growth, although there also may be too much temptation to offset decreasing state support with even higher tuition increases.

Note that one reason to encourage enrollment growth on branch campuses is the fact that their infrastructure and support costs are much lower than at the main campus. Even if tuition is lower than at the main campus, net revenue from branch campus programs may be higher.

A SCRATCH YOUR HEAD EXAMPLE

It would be inappropriate for me to call out specific institutions for which I've served as a resource or consultant. However, I can describe a composite that illustrates the sort of situation that makes me wonder how an institution's branch campuses survive at all. Keep in mind that branch campuses were established for a variety of reasons, and at the time of creation, issues such as we face today were not necessarily a consideration. Rather than emphasizing enrollment growth, it is more likely that branch creation was done with more concern for control than for growth empowerment.

Let's assume that public University A receives state support in the form of a direct allocation and that support has been declining, to the point that the biggest single funding source is now student tuition. University A has two satellite/branch campuses that were established in the 1970s. Although enrollment is more or less flat at the main campus, branch enrollment has increased moderately over the past five years.

Each branch campus has an on-site director, who reports to an associate provost. The director has a modest budget to cover building and grounds expenses, as well as to support a small office staff and local operating expenses. There may or may not be an assistant director, who works with main campus academic departments to build and staff course offerings.

The few resident faculty members are hired and assigned their teaching duties by their main campus department chairs, and those chairs also assign adjunct instructors or main campus faculty members, most of whom teach by interactive television. Separately, University A offers a scattering of online courses, which too often compete directly with on-site offerings. Online revenue is credited to the continuing education unit, and departments receive a few dollars, as an incentive. However, because there is no relationship between the online and on-site courses, cooperation in student advising is not high, and there surely is some cost inefficiency.

The campus directors report constant frustration with trying to meet student needs. Some chairs do a good job, but others take a cavalier attitude toward branch course availability, because they see the branches as a drain on resources and a source of irritation to faculty members.

Chairs will tell you, if you ask, that they do what they can, but they are not going to force anyone to teach courses for branch campus students, and they aren't going to create registration problems for main campus students in order to expand sections on the branches. Too often, the faculty members who agree to teach are the ones who most need the money, and far too often those same faculty members insist on days or times that suit their personal needs, rather than the needs of students. To be sure, there are exceptions, but even a few poorly planned or scheduled classes can severely hurt the ability of branch campuses to fulfill their mission.

By the way, the branch marketing materials claim that the undergraduate business major is available, but there is a required course that has not been offered on campus in over two years. Students are advised to commute to the main campus, seventy-five miles away, for the course, but the class is offered in the evening only once a year, and demand exceeds the seats available.

Bottom line, branch campuses exist in an increasingly competitive environment, and letting critical decisions be made at the main campus is not helpful. At the very least, the branch administration needs a fund to support adding sections of required courses or to meet demand from growth in enrollment. The provost has been considering just such a proposal for the past six months.

A LITTLE ADVICE

Where does all this leave branch campuses? If entrepreneurship and growth are the goals, then the approach to branch budgets is critical. There is a world of difference between a modest effort to extend an institution's reach—an effort that is both tentative and intended to minimize risk—and a serious effort to be competitive in a rapidly changing environment.

If I have an opportunity to advise presidents and provosts, I emphasize three key ideas. First, assuming the institution is not practicing responsibility-centered budgeting, and main campus units receive what I call "expenditure budgets" (annual allocations that create spending targets), please do not apply this approach to branch campuses. Instead, fund them as you would an auxiliary, crediting income generated by their enrollment directly to them. Create an overhead charge that is realistic, so that money begins to flow *from* the branch *to* the main campus, instead of the other way around. As enrollment and revenue grow, the overhead paid should be yoked to that growth.

Second, if you are making what I consider to be the most elementary of mistakes, and placing some or all of the funding for branch instruction in the budgets of your academic units, stop it! The surest formula for discouraging branch growth is to deny branches the ability to develop a course schedule that meets the needs of their students, while expecting main campus chairs and deans to decide which courses are needed on both the main and branch campuses.

If you reverse the flow of dollars, so that revenue flows to the main campus, then adding classes at the branches to support growth will occur more naturally. (I'm not saying that the academic units shouldn't have some level of oversight regarding branch coursework and hiring of instructors, but that the direction in which money flows will tend to drive decision making.) Developing some type of revenue-sharing model, such as our splits approach, will further incent academic units to support increased branch enrollment.

Third, beware of main campus greed. Entrepreneurship requires reinvestment, and for branch campuses to thrive, they need to excel at providing value for their students. That includes utilizing both traditional and hybrid delivery of courses, as well as outstanding student support services. Trying to operate "on the cheap" will interfere with growth, and thinking of branches as "service centers" for main campus academic units completely misses the direction in which programs for adult and other placebound learners are moving.

Looking to the future, I recommend maintaining a strong link between your branch campuses and your online programs, both structurally and financially. During my years as vice president, I considered the fact that I had the branch campuses and the Division of Lifelong Learning in my portfolio to be a major strength. I didn't have much success in building partnerships between the two areas of responsibility, but I did have some control over the use of resources and could prevent direct competition, while making investments to encourage growth in all areas. Those units are no longer linked at Ohio University, at least partly because of the redirection of the old Lifelong Learning unit toward online learning, but I'll say more about that in the next chapter.

9 Lessons Learned
Leadership on and in Support of Branch Campuses

IN THE FINAL TWO CHAPTERS, I WILL review some lessons learned, and then offer thoughts on the future of branch campuses. I view the chapters as related, with an element of summary, so points made in earlier chapters reappear.

Given my interest in organizational behavior, these chapters could easily become books in themselves. I've often said that my years in administration were like having a laboratory for testing ideas. However, I've limited myself here to a short description of key points related to the success of branch campuses—in the present and in the future—and invite others to draw their own conclusions.

To be sure, what I have to say is a product of my personal experience, and although I may have had broader experience with branch campuses than most people, there is no reason to suppose that I have a complete perspective on all the circumstances that contribute to their success. I assume that growth in enrollment is an essential objective for any branch campus and that such growth will come primarily from adult learners and current nonconsumers of higher education. Regardless, for reasons that I will emphasize in the next chapter, I also expect branch campuses to face serious challenges going forward, and their success is by no means guaranteed.

EMBRACE THE HEDGEHOG

Lesson number one draws from Collins (2001): Branch campuses have an enormous advantage when it comes to pursuing their mission, because they are (or should be) hedgehogs, doing one thing especially well (see chapter 3). They do not, typically, provide all the programs and services available at the main campus; they do not have all the infrastructure costs; and even if they encourage faculty research, teaching is clearly the primary mission. Branch leaders should take care to consider seriously how any new program or service fits with the specific campus mission, and they should resist simply trying to replicate the opportunities available at the main campus.

Many of those "foxy" main campuses are headed for very difficult times, if they aren't there already, and that is one of the reasons that presidents want to see more revenue from outreach programs. In the years to come, if branch campuses stick to their mission and make sure they provide value through the way they deliver courses and support students, they may continue to thrive. However, there also is an implication that trying to be too much like the main campus could increase the cost of operation and decrease their attractiveness to the audience they can best serve.

As a side note, focusing on the core mission does not negate the fact that individuals working on branch campuses may have other, personal goals. Moreover, campuses may bring additional services to their communities, concerning perceived needs related to economic development, the arts, healthcare, or school performance. Nevertheless, focusing on the branch campus mission will lead to better hiring practices, more services that make a demonstrable difference to recruiting and retention, and more efficient decision making about new programs.

MANAGING ESTABLISHED PROGRAMS IS DIFFERENT THAN LEADING NEW INITIATIVES

Where existing programs are concerned, all institutions should be in a continuous improvement mode. Attracting a bigger share of a market the campus already serves, increasing student success and satisfaction, and maintaining cost-effective support functions encourage steady growth and improvement. These days, however, campuses face changing demographics and the intrusion of new competitors, so even the best efforts may have modest impact on growth. It becomes all the more important to dwell in the data, in order to adjust to changing conditions.

I will never argue against taking advantage of the energy that can be found in focusing on the strengths of an institution. However, there are deep differences between effectively managing what Govindarajan and Trimble (2010) call the "production engine" and creating an environment that can support and encourage innovation.

It will always be a fool's game, in any industry, to expect the production engine, which is working hard and making decisions based on historical data, to enthusiastically engage in the entrepreneurial pursuit of opportunities that are inherently experimental, relatively high risk, and lacking in well-defined objectives.

I am one who wants and needs to live in the deep end of the pool, but that is not where most people want to be, or should be. Whereas one can manage the production engine in a more or less traditional way, innovation is all about discontinuities, disruption, and surprises. I become very frustrated with educators who pose as entrepreneurs, when their strategies and tactics demonstrate that their thinking is entirely inside the box.

Innovation calls for institutions to move away from traditional strategic plans toward design approaches to thinking and collaborating (see, for example, Kelley 2001 and Martin 2009). Design approaches encourage an iterative approach to development, or what my staff used to call "implementing as we plan." Design processes also tend to encourage small bets or pilot projects, fully expecting the need to adjust on the fly. Innovators definitely should be immersed in the data, but the goal is to capture a wave before it has even fully formed. Educated guesses replace the hope of prediction based on the past.

Innovation is inherently collaborative and team-based. Financial investment, generally, can be relatively modest, but there must be an investment pool that is dedicated to new initiatives. In most cases, the innovation team should include individuals who bring the experience and skills required to support success, but the members must be protected from getting caught up in the day-to-day work of the production engine. Committees or task forces working at innovation on the side will rarely succeed.

ENGAGED PARTNERSHIPS ARE CRITICAL

In my opinion, most of the interesting opportunities for the future depend on establishing what I call "engaged partnerships," both inside and outside the institution. Internally, branches need strong partnerships with key academic units; and externally, they will need partnerships with other institutions, with employers, and perhaps with other entities to which they can outsource certain tangential services.

Just as administrators need to understand the difference between managing steady improvements in existing programs versus leading innovation and entrepreneurial adventures, they also need to understand that meaningful partnerships are not "vendor" relationships, nor are they based on a modest and perhaps even superficial connection, with one "partner" clearly superior to the other. Engagement requires deep commitment over time, listening carefully to each partner's concerns, building high levels of trust, and actively seeking additional opportunities to collaborate that expand from whatever base was initially established.

Specifically with regard to branch campuses, I am especially concerned about the tendency to treat branches as nothing but service centers, extending whatever courses and programs the main campus provides. Especially as the competitive environment changes, institutional leaders should insist that academic units and branch campuses collaborate as partners, in order to more fully understand and exploit local opportunities.

Established branches, if they have pursued their mission effectively over time, have accumulated experience and knowledge that is every bit as critical to building enrollment as is the oversight provided by academic units to assure high quality. As respected partners, branch campus leaders should have a legitimate opportunity to identify community educational needs and should expect the main campus academic and administrative service leaders to seek ways of meeting those needs.

Externally, the principles of engaged partnership are equally important. I'm proud of the community college partnership program we created in my last few years at Ohio University, although it was designed to link community college graduates to online completion programs more than to branch campuses. Partnerships with primary and secondary schools, with employers, and with chambers of commerce all can become substantial and build support for branch campus growth.

INSTITUTIONAL POLITICS DEMAND ATTENTION

Colleges and universities are political institutions, at least in the sense that it is rare for individual stakeholders to have enough power to force their preferences on others. I do think that universities are becoming more "top-down" than they used to be, and I know examples of community colleges and small nonprofits that are run as personal fiefdoms of the president. However, for the most part, complex institutions require that people find ways of working together if they are to succeed.

One implication of living in a political environment, then, is that successful leaders are skilled at building relationships. There is a vast literature examining how we can build strong relationships, even with people we perceive as competitors or "enemies." It is counterproductive to build walls or fences to separate elements of an institution, when cooperation is required for success.

I once heard a branch campus dean say, "I know I should invest time in getting to know people at the main campus, but I'm just not interested." I can appreciate the desire to get on with things at one's own campus, but the problem is that we tend to respect people we know and with whom we spend time. To put it bluntly, strong interpersonal relationships within a branch campus, between branch campuses and the main campus, and between branch campuses and the communities they serve are essential to advancing the mission.

NEGOTIATION SKILLS REQUIRE BRINGING SOMETHING TO THE TABLE

Beyond building relationships, and presumably presenting oneself as a thoughtful person with positive values, negotiation skills are essential in maintaining engaged partnerships. As much as we academics might enjoy debate and attempt to persuade others to adopt our point of view, effective negotiation requires listening well to understand the interests of those with whom we seek productive ties.

Earlier, I wrote about the advantages of interest-based bargaining (Fisher, Ury, and Patton 2011). Another label for this approach is "mutual gains bargaining," which implies a commitment to collaborative, win-win solutions, rather than competing as if we are in a zero-sum game. I learned a long time ago that collaboration often increases the size of the pie, and when that happens, everyone's life is easier. Moreover, negotiations feel much better when we sincerely try to understand other people's concerns, and when they listen to ours.

When we take an interest-based approach to bargaining, with appreciation for the advantages of long-term engaged partnerships, things begin to come together. Ideas can be batted back and forth in an atmosphere of trust, preparing the ground for creative solutions to complex problems. I've experienced competitive negotiations, and I can be firm when necessary, but the pleasure and satisfaction that comes with collaboration is healthier and more satisfying.

That said, successful negotiation also requires that each party bring something to the table. If one party has all the power and control, then concern for mutual gains is unlikely. When negotiation occurs between a branch campus and the main campus, we know that the main campus has history, perhaps formal structure, and certainly control over academic programs on its side. The president may insist on fair solutions, or outside political pressure may force people to the negotiating table, but when push comes to shove, the branch campus may wind up depending on the goodwill of main campus leaders, rather than having the clout to insist on equitable solutions that respect the interests of both parties.

In my experience, money was what gave us negotiating power. The money we earned (primarily from student tuition and state support) came to the branch campuses. As described previously, we paid an overhead to the main campus, but we also were free to develop revenue-sharing agreements, in order to encourage support for those courses and services we needed. At Ohio University, I believe we made an art of revenue sharing, to the benefit of the branches and of the main campus.

So long as branch campuses are "branches" and not independent institutions, they will never control the decisions of main campus academic units. I feel strongly that our control of a scarce resource (money) made all the difference in the world. Thus, I always urge institutions to credit revenue generated on branch campuses to those campuses, then encourage academic departments to benefit financially only to the extent that they serve branch students. I also encourage administrative support offices to make a case for a share of revenue that is tied to *dedicated* support of branch students and operations.

REVENUE-SHARING AGREEMENTS PROVIDE THE FUEL FOR COOPERATION

It follows from the previous section that revenue-sharing agreements are a powerful tool to support the interests of branch campuses. I have never met the dean of a college or chair of a department that would prioritize branch campus courses and staffing over the needs of the main campus—unless there was a clear financial incentive to encourage branch offerings.

If the core activities of the main campus represent the production engine of the institution, then program and delivery innovation is much more likely to come from its branch campuses, online learning unit, or other more or less independent groups that are unencumbered by the need to serve the status quo. It is up to institutional leaders to provide incentives that are valued by the production engine, if innovative programs are to reach their full potential. And that brings us back to the fundamental importance of money.

Deans and department chairs support activities that benefit their units. Although that certainly includes a desire to build and maintain high-quality programs and a strong reputation outside the institution, it also most definitely includes a need for revenue generated outside their unit's normal budget, especially in difficult financial times.

If branch campus enrollment growth is a goal, then the right courses and programs must be available to students at times and through delivery modes that meet their needs. When money flows from branch campuses to main campus units, based on the extent to which those main campus units have contributed to generating revenue, then departments and colleges tend to be more concerned about meeting the needs of branch campus students.

Not incidentally, if revenue flows from the branches to the main campus, and outside the annual operating budget, the institution has, in effect, put the risk for generating that revenue on the branch campus leadership instead of on the main campus unit heads. That is precisely where the risk should be, in line with the expectation that the branch campus should be a place of innovation and entrepreneurial effort.

SOME THINGS NEED TO BE CONTROLLED LOCALLY

This one is absolute: Certain functions should *always* be managed locally, rather than from afar. With regard to branch campuses, the local leadership should be responsible and accountable for marketing and recruitment, for admissions counseling and academic advising, and for developing and staffing the schedule of courses. *These functions will never be performed as well by staff appointed and dwelling at the main campus. Never!*

Leaders of the institution should hold branch campus leaders accountable for making sure that these functions are performed with excellence, assuming appropriate budget and staffing. If there are multiple branches, then some coordination by a central office may help with cost control, with resolving interdepartmental conflicts, and with sharing good ideas. I also can understand establishing a dotted-line relationship between main campus department heads and branch staff performing specific functions. Nevertheless, the idea that the main campus can effectively direct marketing and recruitment, the on-site delivery of support services, or the scheduling of courses is bizarre and wrong.

In contrast, branches generally should rely on main campus offices for registration, financial aid needs assessment, billing, or other functions that are out of students' sight. However, both branch campus and main campus leaders should keep in mind that branch students have definite options and high expectations for good service. Adult learners, in particular, will not tolerate being jerked around. It follows that main campus staff members who also serve branch students need to understand the differences and not expect students to adjust to their main campus preferences. It's about the students, wherever they may connect to the institution.

CULTURE COLORS EVERYTHING

As I wrote earlier, it was stunning to me to discover how different the cultures were between Ohio State Mansfield and Ohio University Lancaster. These were similarly sized regional campuses of public research universities in the same state. In my opinion, a big part of the difference tied to the fact that academic departments hire and tenure faculty members at Ohio State, whereas the individual campuses hire and tenure at Ohio University. But many things drive institutional culture: the nature of how and why the campuses were created, how they are funded, how they perceive mission, and (very importantly) where they are located, among many, many more influences.

When I became vice president, I discovered that the five branches of Ohio University each had their own cultures, as well. Moreover, even as there were retirements among faculty and staff, and as deans came and went, the cultures tended to stay pretty much the same. I think the campuses reflected qualities of their communities, characteristics of long-serving deans, and distance from the main campus.

On the whole, budgets and spending practices at branch campuses in Ohio weren't all that different from one institution to another, but many other practices were very different. Considering the two institutions where I served, Ohio University faculty carry significantly higher teaching loads than Ohio State faculty, but Ohio faculty also have a history of teaching a lot of overload courses, on top of their regular loads. Research expectations and accomplishments are much higher on Ohio State's campuses, and I would argue that, in general, the culture on Ohio State's branches is more like that on their main campus than is true at Ohio, despite the fact that Ohio was the one with a central office on the main campus.

AND A FEW THOUGHTS FOR BRANCH CAOS

The job of a chief administrative officer (CAO) of a branch campus is always challenging, regardless of whether the campus is a small outreach center or a relatively large operation, with several buildings, dozens of faculty members, and a wide range of services. CAOs, like everyone else associated with branch campuses, nearly always feel underappreciated by the main campus leadership They often are frustrated by academic and administrative department heads, even if the president has made it clear that branch growth is a priority. Most CAOs lack the budget authority I enjoyed, and even getting a marketing piece approved or a needed course scheduled at the appropriate times can detract from savoring the fact that their work helps create important opportunities for people who may never have believed that higher education was an option for them.

Leadership success tends to be a result of personal qualities more than of position authority; if you have to fall back on "Because I said so," you are in trouble. Don't fantasize that you are the equivalent of a president—build relationships with other people who influence opinion on your campus and in your institution. What you accomplish will depend on relationships and strong negotiation skills.

On the other hand, unless your campus is quite small and limited in its mission, you should not be treated as a site manager, with virtually no say on important academic and support matters. Your knowledge and experience should contribute significantly to strategic decisions about course and program development to serve your specific audience. You won't always win, but you should ask for and expect a seat at the table on decisions that affect your campus.

In the complex world of branch campus leadership, remember that competence trumps everything else. Regardless of your predilections, go deep on budgets and enrollment data. Frankly, too many CAOs are not well informed on the data that drive their world. Along with deep knowledge of curriculum and course schedules, work to understand all you can about enrollment and what I call the "dynamics" of your budget.

Finally, if you are a branch campus CAO, I hope you have a "number two" on whom you can count. Except for the smallest campuses, branch administration is complex enough that it is important to have that person with whom you can kick around ideas in confidence, as well as to have someone who can step up when you are away. (And CAOs tend to be off campus a lot!) My hope for you is that you have a number two whose strengths and interests complement your own. If the two of you share a vision, but also bring distinct leadership qualities to the campus, you both are truly blessed. I was fortunate to have that sort of connection when I was an associate dean and a dean, and it made all the difference in what we achieved.

In my opinion, the top position on what I've called an idealized branch campus presents an extraordinary leadership opportunity. The size of most campuses means that you can develop a personal relationship with faculty and staff; you can communicate a vision, build community relationships, and help create extraordinary opportunities that will change lives. It is rarely easy, but it is definitely worthwhile.

It is common for new CAOs, especially if they lack previous experience with branch campuses, to quickly realize that they are in an unusual environment. Unfortunately, you won't find a lot of reading material (besides this book!), but there are a few resources worth pursuing. Two relatively recent articles are by Shaw and Bornhoft (2011) and gossom and Pelton (2011). You might also find a volume edited by Samuel Schuman, *Leading America's Branch Campuses* (2009), to be helpful. It has a number of nice case studies and thought pieces.

I also encourage branch leaders to check out the National Association of Branch Campus Administrators (NABCA), at www.nabca.net. Their annual conference is like a group therapy retreat, and on the website you'll find tabs for additional resources. The annual Regional and Branch Campus Administrators (RBCA) conference also provides a supportive, fun environment in which to meet other leaders. (You will find a connection to RBCA on the NABCA site.) Some states have regional or branch campus organizations, including Florida, Ohio, and Oklahoma.

Finally, although it feels self-serving to mention it, I have a branch campus blog, which can be found at www.branchcampus. blogspot.com. Having become a certified professional coach, I also see the value of finding someone outside your own institution who is a good personal fit to work with you as a trusted advisor. Coaches can be valuable thought partners during your transition to a new job or as you develop new initiatives.

10 Future Challenges and Opportunities

TO THIS POINT, I'VE TOLD A STORY ABOUT branch campuses—especially branches of public universities—primarily through my personal experiences, conversations, and observations. Essentially, it has been an idiosyncratic history of branch campuses as I've known them, but along the way I've shared thoughts on the processes, structures, and relationships that contribute to campus growth or that tend to interfere with growth.

Looking to the future, it remains important to understand the history of branch campuses, but it is equally important to understand how conditions in higher education may be changing in ways that could affect the role and the success of branch campuses. In this final chapter, I will offer my sense of where things may go, recognizing that "futurists" are nearly always wrong in detail, and that elements outside the control of institutions may have bigger or smaller effects around the country.

When I look to the future, two broad sets of issues stand out. First, the financial challenges faced by traditional residential campuses—the main campuses in this story—make the imperative for institutions to attract more enrollment from nontraditional audiences all the more serious. Second, technology is creating new options for delivery that are changing the competitive environment in ways that most people in higher education do not fully appreciate.

In both my writing and my speaking for the past several years, I've emphasized that *demographics, technology, and the preferences of adult learners have combined to create a disruptive environment in higher education.* What follows represents my personal assessment, although it is influenced by frequent conversations with others and routine reading of a variety of books and newsletters. I will offer only a few references, but the interested individual should have no problem finding information bearing on the topics. This chapter also draws on an article I wrote on the future of branch campuses (Bird 2011).

My notion of a disruptive environment is derived from the work of Clayton Christensen (e.g., 1997; Christensen and Eyring 2011). Especially in his 1997 book, *The Innovator's Dilemma,* Christensen provides excellent examples of how disruptive innovations led to permanent changes in various industries, often driving previously dominant players out of business. The question for many of us in higher education is whether technology, in particular, but also demographic shifts and the need to recruit more adult learners, have, in fact, created a disruptive environment.

In order to stick with the focus of this book on branch campuses, and to avoid getting dragged down by detail, I will use a bulleted approach to present my key statements. In addition to Christensen's work, I also recommend that readers take a look at Govindarajan and Trimble (2010), *The Other Side of Innovation: Solving the Execution Challenge,* which does an especially good job of explaining the "how" of pursuing innovation. If you read Govindarajan and Trimble, along with Christensen, and perhaps Martin (2009), *The Design of Business,* you will have a very practical understanding of the dynamics involved in responding effectively to disruption. You also will see very little that reminds you of a traditional university.

DEMOGRAPHICS, COST OF ATTENDANCE, AND RELATED POINTS

The following can easily be verified through any number of sources:

- In the United States, the number of young people of traditional student age has been declining and will continue to decline for several more years. There are regional exceptions to this trend, but institutions are fighting over a smaller pie to maintain the size of their first-year classes.

- Importantly, elite privates and flagship publics, on the whole, seek to maintain or to increase the size of their first-year classes. These institutions can hit pretty much any enrollment target they choose, leaving still fewer students available to enroll at other institutions.

- Many institutions are reaching out more broadly, in a geographic sense, with public universities especially interested in out-of-state students, and nearly everyone stepping up their recruitment of international students. In my opinion, these efforts are expensive and likely to be helpful only in the short term, at best.

- Further compromising their balance sheets, many institutions have taken on excessive debt to support building new facilities, including so-called "resort-style" residence halls, nearly palatial fitness centers, and costly athletic facilities. Deferred maintenance, a result of years of neglect in order to avoid steeper budget cuts, also contributes to debt and required debt service.

- As much as Americans value education, there are signs that the cost of attendance is affecting college choice.

If a student studies at a local community college for two years, then enrolls at a public or private university, the diploma at graduation is exactly the same. Moreover, as students take advantage of opportunities to earn college credit while in high school, the total income for higher education institutions from a completed baccalaureate is likely to fall.

• I believe you will find that the most profitable courses at any institution are those in general education, while the most expensive to offer occur in the majors. If institutions lose a large percentage of their most lucrative enrollments to less-expensive providers, that creates still another negative effect on budgets.

• Families more aggressively seek financial aid for their children, and private nonprofits have a serious challenge created by discount rates that often exceed 40 percent of stated tuition. (The implication for many nonprofits is that the same (or even a slightly higher) number of first-year students yields less revenue than in the past.) Although they may seek financial aid, there is not much evidence that families save significantly to prepare for their children's college attendance, making student loans an increasingly necessary choice.

In sum, a reasonably bright young person can earn at least a year's worth of college credits before high school graduation. He or she can then attend a community college or can take additional general education courses online, meaning that the total cost of a baccalaureate degree can be cut dramatically. This development is occurring at a time when the cost of operating institutions has increased substantially. Taking the country as a whole, this is not a sustainable situation, and I suspect most institutional leaders know that to be true. The higher education business model is broken.

In Christensen's terms, we have overengineered the product. That is, the modern institution has so many "features" that it has become almost prohibitively expensive for many potential consumers/students. When a product has been overengineered in this way, the opportunity for disruption appears.

THE PREFERENCES OF ADULT LEARNERS

Many, and probably most, institutional leaders know that they must find a way to attract new audiences if they are going to thrive. This may include developing more market-focused programs and building stronger ties to key employers, and in this context, "new" may also mean expanded efforts to attract more international and out-of-state students. "New" probably also includes exploring the option of online or hybrid programs, as well as encouraging enrollment growth on branch campuses.

Although it certainly is not a new audience, in this same context, most institutional leaders recognize the benefit of attracting more adult learners, as well as more younger students who either did not plan on going to college or who will make their college choice with price and flexibility as a major consideration. (For convenience, I will stick to the term "adult learner," but please understand that I do not necessarily mean people beyond some minimum age, so much as people who make decisions about education in certain ways.)

An important emerging trend with adult learners is that many of them are more interested in earning various skill or knowledge certifications than they are in earning associate, baccalaureate, or master's degrees. Eventually, they may choose to combine certifications and meet other requirements in order to receive a degree, and when they do, they will expect their chosen institution to facilitate that process.

We know that adult learners are more value conscious than traditional students. They tend to seek programs that prepare them for relatively specific careers in business, education, and healthcare. They are price sensitive and less influenced by brand. (That is, they may pay a little more to attend an institution with a strong reputation, but they won't pay a *lot* more. They are perfectly comfortable rooting for the flagship institution's football team while taking their degree elsewhere.)

We also know that adult learners require more flexibility than traditional students, and we know that even small hurdles can cause them to give up or to turn elsewhere. Flexibility refers to the times when classes meet and how often they meet, but also to the dependability of course offerings, the availability of services, and acknowledgment of their work and family obligations.

These same students tend not to be interested in having a wide range of course options to meet specific requirements, but they will not accept being closed out of required courses, having scheduled courses cancelled, or encountering a frustrating bureaucracy when transferring classes from other institutions. My message to traditional institutions is that adult learners do not have to put up with your gatekeeping and slow-to-change attitudes regarding student services. They have plenty of alternatives.

In my experience, private nonprofits have been especially guilty of creating barriers for adult learners. Too often, they have age requirements, allow enrollment in only certain programs or specially designated courses, and deny access to certain services, among other problems. My impression is that some institutions created a program for adult learners, probably in the mid-1970s, perhaps to serve their local community; but they have not kept up to date, and they probably are too expensive to compete effectively in the future unless they make significant changes.

THE ELEMENTS OF DISRUPTION

Perhaps the most important thing to understand from Christensen's work on disruption is that a new and potentially disruptive "product" typically is perceived to be inferior to the existing, dominant product. On the other hand, it may have features that appeal to people who are current nonconsumers, for whom the presently dominant product is too expensive and not user-friendly.

Thus, for example, everyone might agree that online programs were inferior to traditional face-to-face programs, when they began to appear in a serious way. (We could and should debate what "inferior" means, but that's a topic for another day.) Nevertheless, some online programs thrived, because they were *good enough*, and they brought an element of flexibility that opened the door for individuals who simply would never have enrolled in a more traditional program. As the online programs have grown, many of them also have improved in quality, broadening their appeal to potential enrollees.

Frankly, some people say the same thing about branch campuses. They argue that attending a branch is a compromise, accepting a choice that is inferior to the gold standard of a full-time residential experience. For working adults, however, and for some younger students, the branch met their need for flexibility, by being close to home and, often, by providing more opportunities for evening courses. I also would argue that many branches improved over time, as they developed a deeper understanding of their students and their communities.

Characteristically, then, the disruptive options tend to improve over time and to gain wider acceptance, with the result that this new option begins to move "upstream," attracting customers (students, in the case of higher education) who would have selected the previously dominant alternative in the past.

Very importantly, the disruptive option encourages new financial or business models, which drive down the cost of operations and allow the disruptor to undercut the price of the dominant product. With lower prices, greater flexibility, and rapidly improving quality, the stage is set for dramatic change. Bluntly, why would someone pay the higher price for a traditional product, if the new alternatives were just as good, at least in their eyes?

ENTREPRENEURSHIP

I meet some presidents and a reasonable number of branch campus administrators who are personally entrepreneurial, but for the most part, traditional leaders are too buried in the "production engine" (Govindarajan and Trimble 2010) to respond effectively to disruption.

The production engine represents the processes, procedures, and values of the established institution. In the case of higher education, we can look at the recruitment and admission process, retention and student life programs, registration and bursar operations, and so on. Even more importantly, there are deeply engrained academic processes, which control the appointment of faculty and expectations for their use of time, course scheduling and advising, and so on. Understandably, all of these activities are geared to the traditional mission, not only because of the institution's history, but because that traditional student audience currently drives enrollment, revenue generation, and reputation.

In my experience, financial people in higher education are so risk averse that they instinctively resist anything that I'd call entrepreneurial, because it requires investment without assurance of a return. Moreover, they (and the board of trustees) tend to want to see business plans that are impossible to produce, if the entrepreneurial venture is truly breaking new ground. (Analysis of an emerging market is a tough proposition. Certainly you can collect and study data, but any business plan that predicts outcomes is essentially a work of fiction, and trustees need to know that!)

Moreover, entrepreneurial initiatives must move quickly and change direction nimbly. They are inherently iterative, and therefore need to "fail quickly," as the people who write about innovation frequently say. All of this is very difficult for a traditional institution that is accustomed to slow-moving processes and reliance on historical data. Historical data are worse than useless in a disruptive environment.

For these and other reasons, almost anyone who writes about entrepreneurship and innovation asserts that a well-established organization can respond effectively to disruptive change only by setting up an independent entity that can work outside normal channels. In addition, because the early numbers are likely to be small but to increase rapidly, assessment of the new venture's effectiveness needs to tease out the relevant numbers and not let them get lost in a comprehensive picture of the institution.

Finally, even if the leadership does create a relatively independent entity, its growth actually creates new threats to its continued success. As the new venture develops, the production engine will insist that its processes and practices must be brought back into alignment with the processes and practices of the traditional institution. Failure to do so, the production engine will argue, creates too much risk to the "brand," and the new entity is likely to run amok. (Where have we heard that phrase before?) At this point, unless the president is on board and prepared to defend the new initiative, it is likely to lose its energy and its competitive edge. I call this the "bungee cord effect," and oh, do I have examples of its power.

PUTTING IT TOGETHER

The threat to traditional higher education is real. Fighting over a declining audience of traditional students has proven to be expensive, and with revenue challenges coming from many directions, all but the most financially solid institutions face an uncertain future. Elite private institutions and flagship public universities are likely to do well, but their continued success may also contribute to the shaky circumstances nearly everywhere else.

Unfortunately, I anticipate that less prestigious institutions are in for a rough ride when it comes to recruiting nontraditional audiences. First of all, newly emerged for-profit competitors are rocking the boat, and some of the more elite institutions are getting involved in serving these students. It may already be too late for non-elite institutions to develop anything like a comprehensive program of online options, although I do believe they can do some interesting work in niche markets, if they learn to engage deeply with their audience.

Second, new financial models make it likely that the cost of attendance in online programs will be far lower than the cost of a traditional education. Ironically, this suggests that the "profit margin" on each student will be small, so unless programs are scaled to large enrollment, they won't generate enough revenue to offset deficits created by out-of-control costs of operation on the main campus. Some institutions will become very large, but others will fail to compete and become nonfactors.

Of course, some believe that the "threat" of online options, for-profit ventures, and possible "tuition bubbles" is overstated. So far, students and families have been willing to take on considerable debt in order to finance access to a traditional residential experience, and at least some state legislatures are increasing support for higher education. Nevertheless, in my opinion, there are strong indicators that we will not return to what used to serve as "normal." The options created through technology are simply too attractive to fail, even if we can't know for sure just which of the many new initiatives will win out.

Given all that I've described, institutional leaders are right to consider growth at their branch campuses. Branches are ideal locations for hybrid courses and programs, and there is some evidence that hybrid delivery is more attractive to students and leads to stronger learning outcomes than either fully online programs or traditional face-to-face programs. In addition, in their hedgehog way, branches tend to focus on student support, and it appears that retention to graduation will be an even more significant issue in the future. Finally, although in this book I steered away from discussing branches that deliver a single program, I can see attractive opportunities to create niche-focused branches, especially in urban areas.

Unfortunately, my own sense is that main campus faculty and staff members remain ambivalent about growth on their branch campuses, and they certainly are skeptical about expanding online programs, especially if those programs are highly scalable, as they need to be to generate significant net revenue. Most institutions continue to embed their branches and their online programs in their age-old curricular and funding processes, meaning that progress comes slowly, at best, in a time when some competitors are moving quickly to pursue the critical adult learner audience.

Moreover, adult learners are more discerning consumers than they used to be. If an institution is too expensive, requires too much seat time in most courses, or is slow to evaluate transfer credit or to award credit for prior learning, then a large number of prospective students will move on. Being "student focused" is a very serious matter, and it is the students' point of view on service that counts, not anyone else's.

The production engine cannot and probably should not be charged to serve this audience. If the leadership wants to see significant growth in the enrollment of adult learners, then they should embrace the disruption and understand that innovative, entrepreneurial initiatives require a different mind-set than leading the work of the traditional institution.

RECOMMENDATIONS

Branch campuses no longer have the geographic protection they once had, given a plethora of online options. In addition, many public university branches are finding that aggressive private nonprofits are adding branches in or near their communities, and community colleges are getting into serving markets in ways they previously did not. I suppose this is just another example of institutions fighting over declining markets, but it also illustrates the recognition that adult learners and other place-bound students are a highly desirable audience.

In a disruptive environment, you either compete or go home. Assuming that branch enrollment growth is the goal, there will be no substitute for smart decisions, hard work, and an absolute commitment to understanding the student market the branch seeks to serve. My earlier plea that branch leaders dwell in the data is critical, because there is inherent risk in entrepreneurship, and although you cannot analyze an emerging market as well as you might like, it still is important to study markets and closely follow developments as you proceed. After all, some ideas will work and some will not.

It will come as no surprise that I believe the branch organization should be mostly independent of the main campus. Backroom activities such as registration or financial aid needs assessment can be handled well from the main campus, but decisions about the academic program, course scheduling, and student support must be made "in market." Revenue should be attributed to the campus generating it, and then revenue-sharing models should encourage academic unit partnerships and administrative support units to make branch needs a priority.

I also believe the branch organization should report to the same executive-level position on the main campus as the online organization. I can imagine this being done in several different ways, but neither the president nor the provost should oversee entrepreneurial activities; they cannot bring the necessary focus, and they will inevitably give most of their attention to the production engine. Nevertheless, I recommend linking branches and online programs to encourage cost effectiveness and a collaborative spirit. I can almost guarantee you that the branches and online organizations will not be collaborative unless some-one makes sure it happens.

A critical element in branch growth will be pricing. As eager as the main campus may be to see revenue flowing from its branches, the business model of scalable online programs means that branch tuition cannot be too high; indeed, I think it will need to be significantly lower than on the main campus. Because the cost to operate branches is much lower, it should be possible to charge less and still have a better bottom line. Certainly, we did that at Ohio State and Ohio University. Along this line, I want to reinforce my earlier argument that branches must be thoughtful about facilities and services, as well as staffing and teaching loads.

Branches may be able to charge more than highly scaled on-line programs, if they provide a quality hybrid approach, creating some flexibility on class time, but also assuring personal contact with faculty and easy access to services. Students will not pay a lot more, however, and figuring out what constitutes "a lot" is critical. In an age of social media, word of mouth matters. If students have a great experience and testify to the fact that the program is on target for their needs, then they are more likely to say that it is worth the price. Create unnecessary frustration for your students and price will become all the more of an issue.

One other point in favor of branch campuses: Branches bring a physical presence to their communities and an opportunity to build all sorts of significant relationships. People can see the building(s); faculty and administration, presumably, are a visible community resource. The presence of a campus won't offset a lack of responsiveness to student needs, but it does provide distinctiveness in relation to online providers from elsewhere, and it creates a path of least resistance when prospective students begin exploring their options. Branches also provide a strong base from which to build relationships with employers and political leaders.

Growth in online programs complicates the situation for branch campuses. The latter can be effectively scaled to very large enrollment, driving the cost of course development toward zero, and keeping the per-student cost of delivery and support services modest. Moreover, it may be tempting for people at the main campus to believe that they can replace branch campuses with online options that they control. I believe this is a short-sighted view that misses the difference between the audiences for online and hybrid programs, as well as the other advantages created by a physical presence.

ADDITIONAL THOUGHTS

I learned long ago to ask the question "What if I'm wrong?" I don't think there is any doubt that online and hybrid enrollments will grow, and it is nearly certain that we will see more closures and mergers in the higher education world. Nevertheless, the demise of traditional college campuses has been predicted before, so it is reasonable to question whether anything is really different this time around.

Four caveats seem especially significant to me. First, the power of culture is enormous, and many families continue to believe in that gold standard of going off to college. In my view, the traditional campus business model is broken, but maybe new funding models will emerge and institutions will figure out how to manage expenses while keeping tuition under control. Maybe people will be willing to take on still more debt, beyond any level that seems rational.

Second, the role of government and of accreditors could affect how quickly and broadly new ways of going to college develop. Although accreditors of all sorts strike me as being at least confused and behind the curve, they might create hurdles that make online learning difficult to pursue or that somehow reinforce the advantages of attending traditional campuses. Certainly, legislatures are a wild card, and their willingness to help keep attendance affordable is important. I find it hard to believe that legislatures will allow public institutions to fold and disappear from their districts, regardless of the funding issues.

For all this, even if traditional (main) campuses thrive, online programs are here to stay and branch campuses have a relatively well-established place in many communities. Exactly how institutions use branch campuses and fully online programs to serve different audiences could vary, but surely it makes sense to provide whatever range of options audiences will support. So long as we remember the importance of quality and of managing resources effectively, encouraging growth at branch campuses and in online programs can only extend the reach of institutions and expand access to educational opportunity.

Third, the future I've described here oversimplifies the higher education world and the options that actually are out there for students. For example, I have largely ignored the fact that there are quite a few urban universities that primarily serve a commuting population and large numbers of adult learners. As usual, I have no data, but I imagine that such institutions have much in common with branch campuses, although without the quality of "branchness" that has dominated this particular story. My guess is that some of the larger urban institutions will compete very effectively through online and hybrid programs, at both the undergraduate and graduate levels.

Finally, multi-institutional systems also may have some distinct advantages. Here, I include systems such as those in North Carolina, Wisconsin, and California; but I also could point to institutions such as Indiana University or the University of Minnesota, which have multiple campuses that in some ways resemble a main-campus-with-branches institution but also give individual campuses much more independence than branches typically enjoy.

I could go on, but inevitably a book like this one, relying so much on the author's personal experience, must miss

some important distinctions. Nowhere have I discussed the recent trend of American universities opening branch campuses in
foreign countries; nor, obviously, have I considered the relationship between universities and branch campuses elsewhere around
the world, although I know they exist, and I've visited a few.

There is no question in my mind that branches can thrive in the
emerging higher education world, but to do so institutions need
to be thoughtful—strategic—about their role. Indeed, if I were a
president or member of a board of trustees, I'd be genuinely excited about the leadership opportunity to combine the potential
of the main campus, branch campuses, and online programs.

Structure matters, and it is critical to unleash the creativity
that comes with aggressive entrepreneurship. Unless branches
are given the opportunity to engage deeply with their communities, to make sure that the programs offered are the programs
needed, and to stay focused on the access mission, they will
struggle against the competition from other providers. Unless
branches have the opportunity to use the revenue they generate
to motivate strong internal partnerships with academic units,
no one at the main campus will consider them a priority.

As skeptical as I am that most institutions can balance their
budgets serving traditional audiences, I still believe that the
main campus will remain the "main thing," driving the reputation of the institution and bringing critical academic oversight
to assure commitment to high standards. I don't see culture and
politics changing in that regard, but they must not be allowed to
block the ability of branch campuses to pursue their legitimate
mission.

I enjoy speculating about the future, and a big-picture view
that goes beyond the scope of this book is important. I also enjoy
contemplating the idea that those who get it will thrive and
those who do not will fade. We live in interesting times.

References

Bird, C. P. 2003. "Regional Higher Education." In *Ohio University: The Spirit of a Singular Place*, edited by Betty Hollow, 150–52. Athens: Ohio University Press.

———. 2011. "A Perspective on the Future of Branch Campuses." *Metropolitan Universities* 22 (1): 65–78.

Christensen, C. M. 1997. *The Innovator's Dilemma*. Boston: Harvard Business School Press.

Christensen, C. M., and H. J. Eyring. 2011. *The Innovative University: Changing the DNA of Higher Education from the Inside Out*. San Francisco: Jossey-Bass.

Collins, J. 2001. *Good to Great: Why Some Companies Make the Leap— and Others Don't*. New York: HarperCollins.

Dengerink, H. A. 2001. "Institutional Identity and Organizational Structure in Multi-campus Universities." *Metropolitan Universities* 12 (2): 20–29.

Fawcett, N. G. 1984. Interview. In The Ohio State University Oral History Project. http://hdl.handle.net/1811/29290.

Fisher, R., W. Ury, and B. Patton. 2011. *Getting to Yes: Negotiating Agreement without Giving In*. 3rd ed. New York: Penguin Books.

Fonseca, J. W., and C. P. Bird. 2007. "Under the Radar: Branch Campuses Take Off." *University Business* (October). http://www.universitybusiness.com/viewarticle.aspx?articleid=924&p=1#0.

Fuller, C. 2012. *Systems of Postsecondary Education Institutions Reported in the IPEDS Institutional Characteristics Component*. U.S. Department of Education. Washington, DC: National Postsecondary Education Cooperative. Retrieved November 17, 2013, from http://nces.ed.gov/npec.

Gladwell, M. 2000. *The Tipping Point: How Little Things Can Make a Big Difference*. New York: Little, Brown.

gossom, j. g., and M. D. Pelton. 2011. "Branch Campus Leadership: Like Running a Three-Ring Circus." *Metropolitan Universities* 22 (1): 30–47.

Govindarajan, V., and C. Trimble. 2010. *The Other Side of Innovation: Solving the Execution Challenge*. Boston: Harvard Business Review Press.

Harms, Brenda K. 2010. *Up to Speed: Marketing to Today's Adult Student*. Cedar Rapids, IA: Stamats.

Kelley, T. 2001. *The Art of Innovation*. New York: Doubleday.

Martin, R. 2009. *The Design of Business: Why Design Thinking Is the Next Competitive Advantage*. Boston: Harvard Business Review Press.

New England Association of Schools and Colleges Commission on Institutions of Higher Education (CIHE). 2013. Policy on the Review of Off-Campus Programs. Retrieved November 17, 2013, from http://cihe.neasc.org/downloads/POLICIES/Pp27_Policy_on_the_Review_of_Off_Campus_Programming.pdf.

Nickerson, M., and S. Schaefer. 2001. "Autonomy and Anonymity: Characteristics of Branch Campus Faculty." *Metropolitan Universities* 12 (2): 49–59.

Schuman, S., ed. 2009. *Leading America's Branch Campuses*. Lanham, MD: Rowman and Littlefield Education.

Shaw, K., and S. Bornhoft. 2011. "Community Support and Community Relevance to Community: Indispensable Underpinnings for Branch Campuses." *Metropolitan Universities* 22 (1): 13–29.

About the Author

Dr. Charles Bird is Vice President for University Outreach Emeritus at Ohio University. Across a career of more than thirty-five years, he has served as a faculty member and regional campus associate dean at Ohio State University, and as a regional campus dean, vice president and vice provost at Ohio University. Since 2008 he has worked as a consultant, executive coach, and speaker on topics related to branch campuses, programs for adult learners, and leading innovation in higher education.

Dr. Bird holds a BS in psychology from Virginia Tech, and an MS and PhD in experimental psychology from Florida State University. He is a certified professional coach and maintains two blogs: Branch Campus Life, at www.branchcampus.blogspot.com; and Creating the Future (a blog dedicated mostly to positive psychology and "thriving in the second half of life"), at www.drcharlesbird.com/creatingthefuture.

Additional information on Dr. Bird's background and interests can be found at www.drcharlesbird.com. Contact him at bird@ohio.edu.

Made in the USA
Columbia, SC
17 July 2017